# East Midlands Voices

### Edited by Luke Chapman

First published in Great Britain in 2015 by:

 Young**Writers**

Remus House
Coltsfoot Drive
Peterborough
PE2 9BF
Telephone: 01733 890066
Website: www.youngwriters.co.uk

Printed and bound in the UK by BookPrintingUK
Website: www.bookprintinguk.com

# FOREWORD

Here at Young Writers our defining aim is to promote the joys of reading and writing to children and young adults and we are committed to nurturing the creative talents of the next generation. By allowing them to see their own work in print we believe their confidence and love of creative writing will grow.

*Out Of This World* is our latest fantastic competition, specifically designed to encourage the writing skills of primary school children through the medium of poetry. From the high quality of entries received, it is clear that it really captured the imagination of all involved.

We are proud to present the resulting collection of poems that we are sure will amuse and inspire.

An absorbing insight into the imagination and thoughts of the young, we hope you will agree that this fantastic anthology is one to delight the whole family again and again.

# CONTENTS

# THE POEMS

# At The Zoo

I saw a beaming bear babysitting a boring badger,
I saw a babbling barn owl barking at a boring baboon,
I saw a delicate duck dashing towards a dirty dog,
I saw a depressed dog delivering a deaf deer,
I saw a fearless fox fainting on a fake flamingo,
I saw a fast frog feeding a famous fish,
I saw a mad monkey marrying a mending mouse,
I saw a meerkat mending a massive mountain gorilla,
I saw a perfect panther paddling about,
Then I hurried happily home.

**Ayan Naeem**
Arboretum Primary School, Derby

# The Stranger

Me and my friends, standing in the cold,
Then I realised that one of my friends is old.
In the distance there was a bald man,
Then he said, 'Catch me if you can!'
Then the man had some coffee in his hand,
Me and friends wanted toffee ice cream,
Then sand was in my hand.

**Tyler James Paul Wayman (9)**
Bulwell St Mary's CE Primary School, Nottingham

# School Day

I came to school today
it was a good Friday
I had a good day
well, that's what I say.
It was someone's birthday today
Hip hip hooray!
It was the end of term, yay!
I say it was a great day
oh, and it's May, yay!

**Meah Hatherley (9)**
Bulwell St Mary's CE Primary School, Nottingham

# I Opened The Window

I opened the window and what's in sight?
I see a funny, flashing pie.
I opened the window and what's in sight?
A goofy man with a tie.
I opened the window and what's in sight?
A silly bear on a kite.
I opened the window and what's in sight?
A smart man taking a hike.
I opened the window and what's in sight?
A nice, calm lullaby
I lay down my head and got to sleep
But can I just look out my window?
Just a peek?

**Scarlett Barracks (9)**
Bulwell St Mary's CE Primary School, Nottingham

# Weird People

Some people are weird
Other people are scared
Also they eat a whole block of cheese
They rub a whole bar of soap on their knees.

There was a unicorn flying in the sky
Then it turned into a butterfly
A koala drank some hot tea
And was stung by a bee.

Turn that frown upside down
Go and meet a clown
Go swimming, wait, stop!
Do a belly-flop!

Let's go to the movies,
Buy a smoothie
The movie was sad
The screen got torn
The guy was an all right lad.

Let's do some sports
Go get your shorts
Let's play ping-pong
Or let's sing a song.

Let's go to the bar
In our big, black car.

**Lily Leatherland (9)**
Bulwell St Mary's CE Primary School, Nottingham

# The Random Ones

I was sitting on the loo having a poo,
My mum came in, I screamed and shoved her in the bin,
She lifted her head up out of the bin
But I say, 'Mum, you look like a tin,
But I think I will have you for my din . . .'

**Nikkaya Campbell (9)**
Bulwell St Mary's CE Primary School, Nottingham

# Evacuate

Us evacuees, marching to the train,
getting ready to cry in pain.
The train racing to the countryside,
finally we are here.
I want to hide,
waiting to be picked,
but some people are strict.
Staying safe, staying healthy,
The someone chose who was wealthy.
Then one day, planes in the distance,
a flash and a ring,
us evacuees screaming in pain,
we run to the Anderson shelters
where we will be safe.

**Nyle Maltby (9)**
Bulwell St Mary's CE Primary School, Nottingham

# My Strange Cat!

My strange cat, with a pink, twitching nose
doesn't like the garden hose.

As soon as you say water he will run away
and slowly come back the next day.

He is very protective around new cats,
because he's afraid they'll take his beloved baseball bat.

I remember the time when he fell,
so we had to get him out of my neighbour's well.

Yesterday he went all shy,
because he ate my friend's cream pie.

Then at my brother's football match I called his name
and won the game.

And when the Queen was in the canteen,
my cat ran past doing a cheerleader routine.

**Lydia Boot (9)**
Bulwell St Mary's CE Primary School, Nottingham

# The Missing Pants

One day I lost my pants,
then my mum found them,
I said, 'Thanks.'
Then the next day in June or May
another pair flew away.
I was really mad,
so I told my dad
and he found them in his underpants.

**Kayla Lyn Clareece Raynor (9)**
Bulwell St Mary's CE Primary School, Nottingham

# Rocket Launch

R eady for lift-off?
O peration 'Out Of This World' is a go.
'C alling astronaut, do you hear me astronaut?'
K idnapping moon's rock for science is ready.
E xcitement rising,
T hree, two, one . . .

L ift off,
A ll systems go,
U p, up and away.
N ext stop, Moon's surface.
'C ommander, we have our victory,
H ome awaits.'

**Georgina Hessey (11)**
Grace Dieu Manor School, Coalville

# Aliens, UFOs And Planets

A stronauts – Aliens
L ighting up the sky – Neil Armstrong
I n space – Dark hole or black hole
E arth – Pluto
N eptune – Landing on the moon
S pace – Amazing view

U FOs – Night
F ly – End of flight
O rbit – Take-off
S un – Stars.

**Alice-Mae Davison (10)**
Grace Dieu Manor School, Coalville

# Lost In The Universe

Spaceshlp ls flying
Soaring through the universe
Spaceship is landing
Spaceship is on Mars
Spaceship is on Mercury
The spaceship is lost.

**Reims Robert Wright (11)**
Grace Dieu Manor School, Coalville

# Stars

S paceships
T aking off
A ll around.
R ock and soil on a
S tarry night.

**Bo Davis (11)**
Grace Dieu Manor School, Coalville

# Dark But Bright

S pace is so dark and endless
O rigins tell us that
L ights are stars to fill up space
A strologists study space and stars
R eady for something

S tudying our solar systems beyond the Milky Way
Y es – yes, it's true, space is dark but bright out of sight
S hining as we see the past of a star
T rying to shine as long as it can
E xpanding every day
M aybe coming to an end.

**Rupert John Patigas Reeves (11)**
Grace Dieu Manor School, Coalville

# Blank Canvas

On a blank canvas
I can paint a picture
Of Martians and rainbows
Escaped from earthly bounds
Of Saturn and of shining stars
Of barking space hounds.

On a blank canvas
I can paint a picture
Of planets and astronauts
Calling to Houston; home
Of Houston's brave response of
'Sorry Pal, you're on your own!'

On a blank canvas
I can paint a picture
Of aliens and ETs
That float about all day
Of other aliens that party
And float the nights away.

On a blank canvas
I can paint a picture
Of America's flag flying high
On top of the moon
Which in itself, looks like cheese
Or a big, white balloon.

On a blank canvas
That I can call space
I'll complete a beaming sun
That puts everything in place.

**Zara Platts (11)**
Grace Dieu Manor School, Coalville

Congratulations your poem has been chosen as the best in this book!

# Space

Looking at the stars
Looking at planet Mars

I wonder what it's like so far away
I wonder about the Milky Way

'Bedtime,' I hear
'Bedtime,' said Dad, pulling my ear

I sleep with the stars above me
I sleep with the planets above me.

**Sophie Wilson (10)**
Grace Dieu Manor School, Coalville

# The Space Capturer

I will take you away,
With a few Martians today,
Into a dark room
Until the dawn of day.

I will take you down
Till that frown is upside down,
You will cry away
Until my play is a nay.

I'm hidden away,
I'm scared of the Capturer,
But the Capturer
He ain't done today.

**William Marsden (10)**
Grace Dieu Manor School, Coalville

# I Wonder What's Out There

I wonder what's out there,
What could there be?
A black hole, a bus
Or a huge tsunami?
Maybe merchants
From different lands
Or people like my neighbour
With bulging glandes.
I bet they have pets
As strong as bears
And when they go to the barber
They munch on their hairs.
I bet you they're green
Brighter than you've seen
Their teeth are so clean
You can even see them gleam!
Maybe, one day
They will come down to Earth
By the time you know it
They will have given birth.
Maybe that happened
To stunning Lunny
The aliens came down
And made him all funny!
But until later on
We will not know what's out there.

**Max Lewis (11)**
Grace Dieu Manor School, Coalville

# Spaceships

R oar of the engines
O h my, what speed!
C oming through – watch out!
K ey to happiness is
E xploring time and space
T ravelling in your rocket ship

S hooting through dimensions
H urtling to unmarked territory
I ndigo, violet, all the colours of the rainbow
P loughing through stardust
S uch an amazing adventure.

**James Tallett (11)**
Grace Dieu Manor School, Coalville

# Take Off!

Three, two, one, take-off!
Alone in space we fly
Like a kite that's gone too far
Time it will take, but fun we will have

The Solar System floating around
Famous it will become when we land
But for now it's time to fly.

**Madeleine Loader (11)**
Grace Dieu Manor School, Coalville

# Sometimes I Sit And Wonder

Sometimes I sit and wonder
what it's like in space,
how many marvellous planets,
maybe even an alien race?

Sometimes I sit and wonder
how I could even get there.
I might choose a rocket to soar up high,
I know! A flying chair!

Sometimes I sit and wonder
what an alien looks like.
They might be purple or green with spots,
some could be round like the wheels of a bike.

Sometimes I sit and wonder
about the stars above.
They come in fiery red and blazing orange,
some are as white as a dove.

Sometimes I sit and wonder
what I would be able to see,
racing comets and shootings stars,
all a wonder to me.

Sometimes I sit and wonder,
maybe I prefer home.
The huge forests and animal life,
at the beach with fish and sea foam.

**Marley Totton (11)**
Grace Dieu Manor School, Coalville

# Planets

P lanets spinning lazily
L ying in eternal darkness
A ccusing the stars of stealing what
N ever should have been stolen
E ngulfing the attention, hiding
T he true beauty of the
S himmering sun.

**Ben Handford (11)**
Grace Dieu Manor School, Coalville

# Space Poem

Mercury, the smallest planet as a bright object,
beautiful and grey
is here to stay.

Venus, the goddess of love and beauty
is the brightest of them all,
it glows like gold.

Earth is the third planet away from the sun,
the big, blue shaded marble,
different from the rest and is the best.

The sun, the largest star of all,
when it shines that's when I love it best!

The moon, the ruler of the night,
white and bright,
captures the black, dark, shady sky.

**Nikisha Toor (7)**
Griffe Field Primary School, Derby

# Spring Flowers

First sign of spring,
Snowdrops appear,
Like fairy lampshades at your feet

Next come crocuses,
Upside-down raindrops,
In lilac, mauve and amber

Daffodils dance to the bird's song,
Clumps of mustard and gold,
Swaying in the breeze

Like ice lollies of every flavour,
Tulips pop up,
Soldiers standing tall and straight

Fairies' sapphire skirts fill the woods,
The bluebell party begins,
Celebrating spring's last days

Days getting longer,
Spring flowers make way,
For the summer's bright display.

**Lucy Reaveley (7)**
Griffe Field Primary School, Derby


# The Sea And The Beach

At the beach, there are waves splashing in the sea
On a hot day, people are coming to play and having fun
On the sand, people are making wet sculptures
In the sea, fishes are swimming and people are splashing
Under the water, seahorses are swimming and having fun
On the sand, people are finding some little seashells hiding in the
sand
In the sand, people are playing and then going home back to sleep.

**Harjan Rai (8)**
Griffe Field Primary School, Derby

# The Flying Object

Object in the sky -
hovering over, planet to planet,
a cluster of illuminating stars
watch as it slices through the air,
striking with envy.

The stentorian noise cuts through the silence,
what is this oddity?

The black, velvet sky lies unwanted
as all the attention was needed
from the victim.

The celestial wings flew
in perpetual motion.

What was this eerie feature
that lay beyond space . . . ?

**Rhian Kaur Banwait (11)**
Griffe Field Primary School, Derby

# The Peculiar Creature

In a silent, lonely world
Lay a peculiar creature,
Glowing on the vast sphere,
What could it be?
The foreign figure stood,
Confused, scared,
The destructive beast left a stench,
Mumbling curiously,
The misunderstood creature
Started to spin,
Its eyes stuck in position,
What a peculiar creation!

**Stefano Corgiolu (10)**
Griffe Field Primary School, Derby

**15**

# Rocket

There it was!
The vast, metal brute,
It hovered slowly through space,
Conquering many planets.

It roamed the galaxy,
The colossal scrap of steel stole loads of information,
Just like a robber stealing a precious gem,
What is the monster up to next?

Where is it going?
Down it sped towards Earth,
Leaving clouds of smoke trailing behind it,
The high tech machine has disappeared into Earth.
Will the brute return?
Will the spaceship come back
To conquer more than just planets!

**Adam Khan (11)**
Griffe Field Primary School, Derby

# The Sun

Night-breaker
Morning-maker
Human-waker
Summer-lover
Food-cooker
Master illuminator
Paper-burner
Nature-grower
Earth-carer
Space-survivor
Light-creator
Planet King
The sun!

**Oliver Neiland (10)**
Griffe Field Primary School, Derby

## Alien Invader

Lace-like skin,
Disobedient devil,
Vicious mind,
Squeaky voice,
Mysterious language,
Mystical creature,
Deceitful destroyer,
Oxygen-stealer,
Ghostlike moving,
Human-examiner,
Silent creeper,
Phantom features,
Scattered scales,
Alien figure . . .

**Callum Saxon (10)**
Griffe Field Primary School, Derby

## All So Quiet – Space!

All so quiet,
No sound or movement,
A fiery beast,
As big as a dragon breathing fire,
What could this beast be?
5, 4,
Get ready to blast off!
A spaceship!
Eyes light up,
Smoke and fire,
3, 2,1, blast-off!
Zooming into space,
Shooting up to a world of strangeness,
Space!

**Saffrone Gill (11)**
Griffe Field Primary School, Derby

# Alien

Genial figure,
Gloomy mover,
New discoverer,
Mystic monster,
Eccentric beast,
Galactic ghost,
Wondrous being,
Present knower,
Planet ambler,
Gadget user,
Information collector,
Ethical creature,
Technicolour skin,
Mesmerising searcher,
Alien . . . !

**Katie M Humphries (10)**
Griffe Field Primary School, Derby

# Unique Yongy-Boe

Yongy-Boe, a zestful creature,
Has eyes of steel,
Which are biospheres,
Eccentric and brawny,
A kaleidoscope of colours,
Yongy-Boe, a zestful creature,
Cuddly, short and rotund,
The soft, big bear enjoys a zephyr,
Euphoria shows on his patterned face,
Which is wrinkled like a dried apricot,
Arms of jelly attached to his puny body – he was erratic,
A zing alien,
Hydrangea lover,
Riotous fella with a huge heart,
Yongy-Boe a zestful creature.

**Connie Jupp (10)**
Griffe Field Primary School, Derby

# Spaceship

Star-zipper,
Rocket-flyer,
Space-crafter,
Weapon-fighter,
Jet engine,
Above gravity,
Big atmosphere,
Flying asteroids,
Passing Mars,
Charging down,
Planet-orbiter,
Forever exploring.

**Jenna Foxon (10)**
Griffe Field Primary School, Derby

# Planet Of The Aliens!

Zooming spaceship.
Zero gravity,
Floating around,
Green glimpse,
Alien shock,
Foreign figure,
Ghostlike being,
Planet alone,
Strange creature,
Unusual language,
Odd planet,
Mercury-lover,
Timeless trekker,
Exotic aliens,
Spacesuit-explorer!

Do these creatures really exist?

**Ellie Sutheran (10)**
Griffe Field Primary School, Derby

# When The Fuscoferuginous Alien First Landed On Earth

The ravenous beast awaited his friends,
A kaleidoscope of deep colour,
Falling through gravity,
Oh, how much Cuddlebop wished for a home!

Parched, drenched, unkempt,
Wobbling – his legs were jelly,
Jiggling on an emerald plate,
Oh, how much Cuddlebop wished for a home!

Gawky and psychic,
The wisteria alien was very rotund,
As round as a tree trunk,
Would Cuddlebop find a home on Earth?

**Victoria Wandless (10)**
Griffe Field Primary School, Derby

# The Mysterious Alien

Curious creature,
Unknown personality,
Mysterious mind,
Life-drainer,
Planet-conqueror,
Dark destroyer,
Camera shy,
Mars ruler,
Ship hijacker . . .

The unknown alien!

**Sachin Atwal (10)**
Griffe Field Primary School, Derby

## Space Alien

Space alien.
Oxygen-absorber,
Home-searcher,
Mysterious monster,
Insightful learner,
Bountiful helper,
Excited traveller,
Extraordinary experimenter,
Future-seeker,
Long liver,
Space alien . . .

**Madiya Fathima Hussain (11)**
Griffe Field Primary School, Derby

## Space – Out Of This World!

Mystical beast,
Lopsided face,
Vivid colours,
Glaring eyes,
A crater home,
Bizarre beast,
Some good,
Some bad,
Some ugly,
Space-explorer,
One of a kind,
Weird walker,
Sleeky stalker,
Aliens.

**Sarvraj Khunkhuna (10)**
Griffe Field Primary School, Derby

# Spaceship

Zooming stars,
Across the sky,
Mars the planet,
Sun, day and night,
Rocky planets,
Shooting stars,
Planet Earth,
Double star,
Alien planet,
Black hole
Jupiter's moon,
Asteroid belt,
Dwarf planet.

**Georgia Doyle (11)**
Griffe Field Primary School, Derby

# The Mysterious Planet

Gleaming shiner,
Vast floater,
Still slayer,
Nothingness bringer,
Gas giant friend,
Zodiac inhabitant,
Aegir orbit,
Helium sphere,
Astronaut's heaven,
Aurora creator,
Black hole maker,
The mysterious planet . . .

**Sakthi Venugopal (11)**
Griffe Field Primary School, Derby

# The Earth!

Temperature-changer,
So much nature,
A world full of animals,
People making chemicals,
So much life,
That you wouldn't kill with a knife,
Lots of slaughter,
So so much water,
Blue as the sky,
Time to say goodbye,
A blue sphere,
But no fear,
Human-maker,
Ultimate creator,
The Earth!

**Adam Banks (11)**
Griffe Field Primary School, Derby

# The Astronaut Who Travelled To Space!

Silent person,
Spacious rocket,
Quick traveller,
Unknown passer,
Travel-lover,
Space-liker,
Moonwalk-enjoyer,
Moon-lander,
Rocket-driver,
Gravity-hater,
Alien-killer,
Weapon-carrier,
Sky-floater,
Planet-collector.

A spaceman!

**Amelia Marie Treasure (10)**
Griffe Field Primary School, Derby

# The Delightful Discovery!

5, 4, 3, 2, -
Button eyes light,
Rocket boosters blast,
Vehement noise,
1, blast-off!
Skimming through the sky, I spotted an illuminated planet,
floating carelessly under a blanket of blue,
As I landed on the azure crust of the planet,
a Martian was noticed by me,
An alien with great oddity,
A mystifying, inexplicable creature waiting,
waiting to be discovered and loved.
Without warning, an army of spacemen,
no different in appearance than me,
but in personality,
A multitude of colours shot out of the cumbersome guns,
With eyes like daggers and hearts of steel,
they edged closer to the poor creature.
My head spun mercilessly,
I was about to help the Martian when . . .
Hup, two, three, four!
A swarm of aliens fought off the baddies
and made room for the good.
Will you be a malignant murderer or a saving moralist?

## Ihina Painuly (10)
Griffe Field Primary School, Derby

# Space – Out Of This World!

White suit,
Lead boots,
Slow motion,
No oxygen,
Crisp fabric,
Planet below,
Extensive ship,
Spacecraft,
Gigantic windows,
Jet engines,
Air chamber,
Major weapons,
Huge missiles,
Charging fast,
Strange figure,
Weird figure,
Glaring eyes,
Ghostlike
Slimy creature,
Out of this world!

**Lylah Javed (10)**
Griffe Field Primary School, Derby

# The Alien

Galaxy-hopper,
Star-stopper,
Genial being,
Placid creature,
Galactic ghoul,
Mystic Martian,
Secret searcher,
Past-watcher,
Future-seer,
Knowledge-knower,
Planet-scourer,
Technicolour beast,
Misunderstood Leviathan,
Majestic monster,
Information-bearer,
Human-carer,
Life-protector,
Intergalactic life form,
Language-collector,
Asteroid-raider,
The alien . . .

**Emily Davies (11)**
Griffe Field Primary School, Derby

# The Rejected, Unwanted Alien!

A rejected, unwanted alien,
Who was very malicious,
Glowing with envy as he watched,
Sitting, staring with his eyes of granite,
At the other jubilant life-forms,
Sitting, staring with his eyes of granite
At the silhouette of gargantuan plants,
When – *whoosh!*
A capacious rocket was zooming towards him,
Was it an ally? Was it an enemy?
It was zooming towards him as fast as sound itself,
*Crash, bang!*
The spaceship had landed,
Wow! A new friend,
His fingertips reached towards the man,
Shaking, quivering hand,
Yes – he took it!
Bouncing to the interstellar spaceship they got in,
5, 4, 3, 2, 1, blast-off!
The dragon took off with a mighty roar,
What would happen . . .?

**Sophie Price (11)**
Griffe Field Primary School, Derby

# Space

As I gaze down from below
Through my telescope,
I watch the whooshing asteroids
And look up with hope.

I wish that I could go up there
Into the glow of glistening stars,
Through the kaleidoscope of colours
The redness of Mars.

I wish that I could witness
The warmth of the sun,
The orbit of every planet
All of its secrets undone.

I wish that I could float amongst
The rotating rings of Saturn,
The rocky grounds of Mercury
And feel the planet burn.

As I gaze from down below
Through my telescope,
I watch the whooshing asteroids
Still staring up with hope!

**Amrit Dhillon (11)**
Griffe Field Primary School, Derby

# Space

Star-shooter
Comet-thrower
Asteroid-zoomer
Mind-blower
Breath-taker
Rocket-flyer
Colour-blender
Black hole-maker
Flag-holder
Planet-saviour
Wish-giver
Spine-chiller
Moon-spinner
Aliens murmur
Silence-breaker
The beauty
And grace
Of
Outer space.

**Hermarni Gordon (11)**
Griffe Field Primary School, Derby

# Aliens

When I saw this strange alien
I had to inspect and poke . . .
I thought it was a dream,
But I realised it wasn't a joke!

When it started to speak weirdly
And it showed me to its peculiar planet,
Where the air is impure and very filthy
I started to think I'd had it!

When it introduced me to its large family,
I really wondered why,
Until they put me on a table,
I thought I was going to die!

I just about managed to escape
Without a single scratch!
I had to say goodbye
As I had to watch the match.

As I went to bed
I looked up into the sky,
I now just thought
Maybe, we'll again, say hi!

**Jai Shergill (11)**
Griffe Field Primary School, Derby

# Space

Stars twlnkling in the night sky
like fizzing fireworks falling
pictures forming in the sky
like priceless pictures.
Astronauts flying into space
like an eager boy to get a toy.
Cockpits sitting like a boy
sitting in front of a television.
Eclipse forming
like a back hole.

**Oli Worthington (11)**
Griffe Field Primary School, Derby

# The Planets

As I walk free
I see minute Mercury.
A constellation of shining stars
Covering marvellous Mars.

Exotic Earth, full of life,
Violent Venus like a dice.
Spinning Saturn with amazing rings,
Jumping Jupiter throwing things.

Urging Uranus, like a ball,
Petite Pluto, extremely small,
Noble Neptune, we don't know much about,
Maybe learn more and we'll find out.

**Daniel Parkes (11)**
Griffe Field Primary School, Derby

# Astronaut

A mazing asteroids, like vast caves filled with shimmering stardust,
S hooting stars whizzing by as bright as the flash of a camera.
T raumatised Martians creeping over the galaxy, watching the
astronauts explore the meteor.
R uby-red dust filling the air, trying to catch up with the dazzling
stars
O rbiting around the sun, the Earth's blues and greens beginning to
turn emerald and turquoise.
N ine circled planets dancing around the sun, like the first dance at
a wedding,
A ll around the planets, the stars shimmer brighter than a lit fuse,
U nder the stars, as dark as the night sky.
T he planet Pluto as small as a tennis ball.

**Sourav Gill (11)**
Griffe Field Primary School, Derby

# The Life In The Universe

The ship of the night orbited around the sky's candle,
Winter's blade froze the galaxy,
But the warmth of the sun placed a blanket of heat over the universe.

The beautiful light of the stars lit the sky's black cloak,
Pluto sent the sun northern kisses to say, 'Thank you,'
Not knowing that winter's blade could kill her.

She held her planet so high,
It did not affect her,
Every planet lives how they are now
And do not allow winter anywhere close.

**Kia Dickinson (11)**
Griffe Field Primary School, Derby

# The Deep Dark Space!

Stars sparklIng,
Planets spinning,
Sun burning,
Rockets zooming,
Meteorites exploding,
Comets shining,
Black holes expanding,
Astronauts exploring,
Cyclamen colours colliding,
Rough rocks cracking,
That is what space is like.

**Charisma Ashlei Wheeler (11)**
Griffe Field Primary School, Derby

# Flying Out To Space

I'd dream of flying out to space to see the glistening stars,
And the vast amount of flamboyant colours
Illuminating the sky.

I'd gaze, amazed at the radiant sun
Sending colourful beams out through the empty void
And I'd search for rocky asteroids
Falling down with unimaginable speed,
Leaving fiery flames of scarlet and emerald gleam.

I'd glare at Mars, searching for suspicious aliens
And I'd hope that one of them is called Zlien.
I would fly around the rings of Saturn
And I'd stare, fearless next to Jupiter,
I dream to fly to space
Where dreams come true.

**Kieron Sall (11)**
Griffe Field Primary School, Derby

# Castles

Castles are grey and black,
knights live in them.
They are as strong as stone,
there are thousands of castles
that are eight thousand years old.
They weigh one hundred tonnes.
All brave knights fight,
I have seen lots of new and old castles,
kings and queens live in them.
They are really scary
because there are powerful dragons in them.
There are also powerful dragons in them.
Knights ride huge, hot and heavy horses,
huge horses live in secret stables,
the stables are strong as bricks.
Knights have lots of bites
because vampires bite them.

**Varun Punni (7)**
Griffe Field Primary School, Derby

# School!

First we start to spell
I got them all right so I tell.
Next was playtime in the sun
When we were having fun.
Now it is time to start
The very messy art.
Now the cool
Is the school.
My friend has hair that is long
She got most of the answers wrong.
I was bright
So I got all the sums right.

**Sophia Hume (7)**
Griffe Field Primary School, Derby

# The Rocket!

The rocket Is fast lIke a racing car,
It shoots into the air, it is big.
Rockets fly to the moon,
Astronauts go to the moon and they float like a cloud.
The rocket is red, yellow and orange,
They see the planets, Earth and the sun,
Which is very hot.
Rockets have red-hot fire coming out of them!

**Aman Kaur Garcha (8)**
Griffe Field Primary School, Derby

# Ocean

The ocean waves sparkle in the sunlight,
The sea shakes in the dark and gloomy night,

The ocean is beautiful, blue and clear,
It moves on a warm day like an elegant deer.

The sea is graceful on a silent day,
The ocean has a relaxing, gentle sway.

In the evening, the sunset is mixed with the sea and the night,
It's really a very pretty sight.

**Thea Kaur Badh-Drost (8)**
Griffe Field Primary School, Derby

# The Miracle Of Friendship

A miracle called friendship dwells within the herd,
You don't know it happens or when it gets its start.
But the happiness it brings you always gives a special lift,
Then you realise that friendship is one of God's most precious gifts!

**Yusuf Zia (7)**
Griffe Field Primary School, Derby

# Juicy Fruit

Yummy and healthy,
such a juicy fruit.
Green like the grass
and as round as the sun.
*Crunch!*
An apple really fills up the tank.

**Sarah Beth Towle (7)**
Griffe Field Primary School, Derby

# Racing Cars

The cars are like shiny rockets on the
starting grid, revving and waiting.
Suddenly the lights go out and they
all dive into the first corner.
They zoom and zoom into the straight,
wheel to wheel, towards the hairpin.
A driver loses control and the crashing
car spins into another.
The bright yellow flags are waved
and the race continues.
Mile after mile, the cars race neck
and neck into the final lap.
Just then the leader's gearbox blows
and the car crashes into the barriers.
I take the lead
and win the World Championship.

**Harry Dalgleish (8)**
Griffe Field Primary School, Derby

# My Teddy

My teddy is a friend to me,
she dresses up in my clothes,
so my teddy is warm!

She sleeps with me
in my cosy, warm bed
and reads with me!

My teddy and me
always play together
with my best friends.

**Tarahshri Shri Murugan (8)**
Griffe Field Primary School, Derby

# Cupcakes

Baking my cupcakes,
I am excited,
Stirring the mixture,
Watching them rise.

Pink, yellow and green,
What a surprise,
Look at these cupcakes,
Mmm! They are nice.

**Amreece Dhillon (8)**
Griffe Field Primary School, Derby

# Be A Sun Safe Superstar!

When the sun is shining, you need to be a sun-safe superstar,
Remember all the rules and you will go far.

Choose cool clothes, cover your shoulders and chest,
Keep your skin nice and cool and you'll feel the best.

Sun cream will stop your skin from turning pink,
It's time that everybody did stop and think.

Wear a big sun hat and protect your head,
Never let your scalp turn a shade of red.

Sunglasses protect your eyes from the sun,
Sun damage is really not so fun.

When you're outside try and find some shade,
Stay hydrated and have some lemonade.

Sipping water keeps you cool,
Stay hydrated, don't be a fool.

Now you know what to do, you can go and have some fun,
Remember all the rules and you'll be safe out in the sun.

**Blossom Diffin (7)**
Griffe Field Primary School, Derby

# Dinosaur Poem

The glgantosaurus
he was colossal
but in the end
he became a fossil!

Dinosaurs were around
many years ago,
they lived on sea and land,
They lived up high and low.

The gigantosaurus
he was colossal
but in the end
he became a fossil!

People think the land ran out of water,
or a volcano killed them off,
the molten lava and smoke
made them sneeze and cough.

The gigantosaurus
he was colossal
but in the end
he became a fossil!

**Joseph Fleming (7)**
Griffe Field Primary School, Derby

# My Best Experience!

When I sailed out to space,
Many years ago,
I didn't know what to expect,
But now I really know!

I saw . . .
Waves of colours as they wash me
And shooting stars pass by!
But I mustn't forget the time when -
I saw a rainbow in the sky.

When I saw the flamboyant colours
I couldn't believe my eyes!
It was boring and plain on the moon,
So I flew up to the Milky Way, up high.

I dreamt of flying to Venus,
But I heard bad things about it,
Then I jumped on one of Jupiter's moons
And said, 'You'll never get another one of these chances.'

I didn't want to go back to Earth,
But I knew I had to go.
I'd said I'd only be a while to Mum
And she's probably freezing in Alaska's snow!

I have enjoyed this experience very much,
It truly has been great!
My mum might be waiting
And she'll be angry that I'm late.

But I really don't care,
Nothing beats space.
I'll act sweet and cool,
Then walk in with grace!

**Evie Lorenne Humphries (10)**
Griffe Field Primary School, Derby

# Space

As the never-ending blackness stretches across space,
Swarming stars illuminate the dark atmosphere,
These views are to my exquisite taste,
Stars as bright as the crackling sphere.

Magnificent Mars is full of scarlet dust,
However, it is not full of rust,
Marvellous Mercury edges the crowd,
Yet, it is not very loud.

Extravagant Earth, full of life,
Where people like to play with dice,
Super Saturn is surrounded by icy rings
And is full of different things.

Peculiar Pluto, covered in dazzling blue,
Unfortunately it is far off the age of two,
Urging Uranus, smothered in green,
But it is very lean!

Neat Neptune is very cold
And it hadn't been told,
Jolly Jupiter has stunning looks
Which haven't yet been took.

Vile Venus is full of evil,
Obviously it isn't full of eels.

**Manveer Singh Kalirai (10)**
Griffe Field Primary School, Derby

# Space

As I stare up into outer space
With hope in my eyes,
I wish I could go up there one day
And watch the twinkling stars float by.

I wish I could see the kaleidoscope of colours
And the shimmering, sparkling stars.
I wish I could gaze at the suspicious swirls
And the glowing redness of mars.

I wish I could gaze at the rushing asteroids
And the soft fragrance of the night.
I wish I could see the spinning of an enormous meteor
And the amazing dazzling sight.

I wish I could float in the icy rings of Saturn
And witness Pluto's frosty atmosphere.
I wish I could explore Jupiter's sixteen moons
And Mercury's hot rocky grounds.

As I stare up into outer space
With hope in my eyes,
I wish I could go up there one day
And watch the twinkling stars float by.

**Sita Amika Raithatha (11)**
Griffe Field Primary School, Derby

# Space

Amazlng allens
Asteroids falling . . .
Vast and vibrant
Dazzling stars
Miniature Mercury
Black holes everywhere
Luminous colours
Planets orbiting
Cold comets
Stars gleaming
Icy rocks
Giant Jupiter
Miraculous Mars
Gravity nowhere
Mind-blower
Gleaming fireworks
Shooting stars
Peaceful planets
Eclipse-maker
Space-searcher
The calm and peaceful place called space.

**Abhay Gill (11)**
Griffe Field Primary School, Derby

# Flying To Space

As I peer down from space,
I gaze at the stars with great grace.
Twinkling and winking from the stars,
Amazed by the sight of Mars.

Planets far ahead, planets far behind,
I fly past Jupiter which blows my mind.
The icy rings of Saturn and Jupiter nearby,
I stare at the Milky Way, way up high.

Pluto I can't see,
But it still amazes me,
Mercury is quite astounding, the closest to the sun,
It really is astonishing, you should really come!

I have been to many planets . . .
But it's time to say goodbye,
I get into my rocket,
From way up high!

**Emily Yau (11)**
Griffe Field Primary School, Derby

# Space!

Oxygen-destroyer
Deep thinker
Asteroid-flyer
Planet-keeper
Picture-maker
Earth-shaker
Gravity-stealer
Star-wheeler
Bright glower
Constellation shower
Astronaut-floater
Alien-hider
Black hole-creator
Mind-blower
Meteor-thrower
This is space!

### Emily Charlotte Bull (11)
Griffe Field Primary School, Derby

# Through The Telescope . . .

Shimmering, shining, shooting stars,
Stretch out before and after Mars.
I like to wonder what lies there,
In the corners of space, far and near.

Through the telescope I can see
The rocky moon and its radiant beams.
I can see the constellations shine,
Across the area, in a line.

Also, I watch the icy comets
And the rockets.
How I wish to go up to space
And stare at the shooting stars.

I wish to visit the barren planets
And enjoy the view of space.

**Zainab Awais (10)**
Griffe Field Primary School, Derby

# Spectacular Space

I dream of sailing out to space
Watching the glistening stars,
I'd look up to the top
And see the beautiful planet, Mars.

I dream of sailing out to space
Where everything is still,
I'd see the pretty planets,
That would be a thrill!

I dream of sailing out to space
Watching the moon go by . . .
I'd love to touch its rocky surface
Whilst it's in the sky.

I dream of sailing out to space
Which would be the best,
Staying there for ever
Would make my life better than the rest.

**Suneel Singh Dosanjh (11)**
Griffe Field Primary School, Derby

# Space

Mercury is blistering
Mercury is microscopic
Mercury is desolate and deserted
It's just a rocky globe

Venus is surrounded with thick, heavy clouds
That hide what's beneath
The ground is as hot as a furnace
The air is dark and smoky

Mars is very scarlet
Mars is barren and bleak
Someday you might visit it
If you're really brave

Jupiter is enormous
Jupiter is forsaken
It has sixteen moons
And a mammoth crimson spot

Saturn had great, round rings
Now we know what they are
They are just icy rocks
Which astronauts see as gas.

**Hassan Zafar (11)**
Griffe Field Primary School, Derby

# Flying Out To Space

Asterolds
Black hole voids
Rockets, brilliant bright
In constant flight
Stars greet with a wink
Say goodbye with a blink
Planets orbit
As asteroids rotate
In the soothing air
As the luminous stars
Reflect on Mars
Where are Saturn, Uranus, Neptune?
They are away, like the moon
A telescope would be the best
For spotting and the rest.
I look for planets in the sky.

**Jonathan Cooper (11)**
Griffe Field Primary School, Derby

# Flying Out To Space

I dream of flying out to space,
Upon thousands of shimmering stars,
I'd zoom right up to the top of the galaxy
And stare at Jupiter and Mars.

I dream of flying out to space,
In flying saucers and rocket ships,
I'd mingle with the aliens
And discuss our adventurous trips.

I dream of flying out to space
And looking down at the Earth,
I'd be an astronaut for a day before
I have to return to my berth.

I dream of flying out to space
And living there for ever,
But, sadly, in my wildest dreams
It will never happen – never . . .

**Holly Rose Barnes (10)**
Griffe Field Primary School, Derby

# The Greatest Creation

Hollday-booker
Electricity-generator
Ice cream-melter
Sun-tanner
Day-former
Plant-grower
Window-opener
Weather-changer
Barbecue-decider
Water-dissolver
Fruit-creator
Rainbow-former
Holiday home-builder
Life-saver
Fire-starter
Mood-changer
Eye-blinder
Atmosphere-changer

The greatest creation -
The sun!

## Daniel Griffiths (11)
Griffe Field Primary School, Derby

# Peering From Space

As I peer down from space I see . . .

Stars shooting by as fast as lightning,
The golden sun, glowing and brightening,
Asteroids swiftly hurtling through the air,
Zooming past Jupiter, I stop and stare!

A kaleidoscope of fluorescent colours,
Glowing in the night
And silent it is until a meteor dashes by,
Giving me a piercing fright,
Great beauties to be seen,
The moon blinds me with its gleaming beams.

A vigorous rush of wind hits my face,
As a meteor rushes by with grace,
Pluto, Mercury, Venus and Mars,
Twinkling, glistening, faraway stars.

As I peer from Earth I see . . .
Nothing but land, valleys and trees!

**Kimran Gill (10)**
Griffe Field Primary School, Derby

# Sailing Out To Space

I dream of sailing out to space,
upon the shooting stars,
with black holes alongside,
I gaze, amazed, at Mars.

And sailing through the fluffy clouds
I'd wave down to Earth,
thinking of my family
And what it was worth.

All the planets in the air that I just can't bear,
with stars as bright as lights
shining all over the world
and twinkling all night.

I dream of sailing out to space,
being happy with a smiling face!

**Jaya Gill (11)**
Griffe Field Primary School, Derby

# I Wish

I wish of sailing out to space
Where everything is still
Flying high, up in the stars
That's where I belong!

Whizzing past the planets afar
Jupiter, Venus and Mars
Flamboyant colours I can see
What a wonderful sight!

Deeper I fly into emptiness
This world would be the worst
Black holes beckoning me
Into their misty palace of doom!

I wish of sailing out to space
Where everything is still
Flying high, up in the stars
That's where I belong!

**Charlotte Miller (11)**
Griffe Field Primary School, Derby

# My Mum Is The Best

My mum is the best,
My dad is amazing,
My two sisters are good, but silly,
When my sisters are upset, I'm always there for them,
When my mum rests I am always quiet,
When my dad goes to work, I always say goodbye.

**Amrita Badwal (8)**
Griffe Field Primary School, Derby

# Why You Don't Like Mars

There was an alien who once lived on Mars,
He didn't like it there, because there were no cars.

He searched around the planet for something to chew,
But unfortunately, he couldn't find any food that would do.
He couldn't even find water,
It almost felt like torture.

The only reason he likes people,
Is when they come, they bring treacle.

**Luke Banks (8)**
Griffe Field Primary School, Derby

# Black Holes

B lack abyss, soaring to nearby flamboyant planets
L onely, barren, squinting at the Milky Way
A n extraordinary creation sucking everything in its path
C ontaminated, foul air, destroying any form of life
K illing planets with one ginormous suck

H orrifyingly large, even for the Earth!
O nly one can remain . . .
L eaving a booming blast of a supernova
E ternal scars leaving planets devastated
S ombre atmosphere filling the sky.

**Aarondeep Singh Atwal (10)**
Griffe Field Primary School, Derby

# Space

Galaxy exploring
Black holes sucking
Asteroids crashing
Rockets riding
Star gazing
Astronauts researching
Cockpits sitting
Planets orbiting
Moon walking
Meteors zooming
Gravity dragging
Sun heating
Stars shining
Planets spinning
Eclipse watching
What could it be?

Space!

**William Stewart (11)**
Griffe Field Primary School, Derby

# Stars

There was a star,
but not very far.
Stars are bright
like a gleaming light.
A star grants wishes
like a pile of dishes.
All so high
above the sky.

Thousands of people watching the sky
maybe there is one star nearby.
Always having a little star
is it near, or is it far?
By now it's time to say goodbye
when coming back to a starry, night sky.

**Zihan Qin (7)**
Griffe Field Primary School, Derby

# My Pony

I love my pony
He is fluffy and white
Never bony
He eats day and night
Jumping high, into the sky
Sometimes I feel like we fly in the sky
Bobby is the best pony I've ever had
When I ride him, he makes me glad
Riding is my life, nothing makes me happier
Than spending every day in the saddle.

**Lucy Buxton (8)**
Griffe Field Primary School, Derby

# I Love Cricket

I love cricket, hit the wicket,
I like to run, in the sun,
I love footie and you get muddy,
I like snooker, I play it with Luca,
I love to box, but not a fox,
I like tennis, like Jessica Ennis,
I love darts, they make you get the farts,
I like boules, I know the rules.

**James Robert McSherry (7)**
Griffe Field Primary School, Derby


# Who's The Famous Person?

'Who's the famous person?'
I asked my dad, but he doesn't know.
I searched the Internet and everywhere,
Do you know who's the famous person?

There was a loud bang,
Where did it come from,
It's coming from the roof,
Whatever, loud noise is gone . . .

I thought to myself,
*the famous person must be royalty.*
I am nutty, so I must be
The famous person.

**Sourish Arun (8)**
Griffe Field Primary School, Derby

# Stars

I see them brightening the sky,
Too many to count,
Beside then is their neighbour, the moon,
Glowing like a bright, light ball in space,
The stars are like tiny holes poked into a sheet of black paper,
They're so far away, I wonder how they still shine so brightly,
I hope that you'll be there for ever
And that you'll never go away.

**Nathan Namgoong (7)**
Griffe Field Primary School, Derby

# Penguins

Penguins are black and white,
they have perfectly good sight.

Penguins have got long, thin flippers
and webbed feet that look like slippers.

Penguins waddle when they walk,
I find it funny when they talk.

Penguins live at the South Pole,
where winters are snowy and freezing cold.

**Zayn Raja (8)**
Griffe Field Primary School, Derby

# Chicks

C hirping chicks playing together
H appy chicks running about
I n the incubator, keeping warm
C uddling up together, safe and sound
K indly sharing all the food
S leeping soundly, huddled together.

**Emma Rose Barry (8)**
Griffe Field Primary School, Derby

# My Annoying Sister

My sister is annoying,
doesn't anyone understand?
She really got me this time
and she is only nearly nine!

My sister is annoying,
it always happens to me.
Why can't it be my sister?
She always embarrasses me!

My sister is annoying,
She can't stop kissing me,
she kicks and punches, screams and shouts,
but Mummy always believes me.

My sister is annoying,
but she's someone I couldn't live without,
it gets me all the attention,
but I love her just the way she is.

**Luca Carratu (8)**
Griffe Field Primary School, Derby

# The Flowers And Trees

The flowers and trees are very pretty,
If they were gone, it would be a pity,
Tulips and buttercups are very bright,
Roses and daisies are like a light.

### Jack Williams (8)
Griffe Field Primary School, Derby

# Leaves

Little leaves on the ground,
Little leaves swaying round,
To the wind and the breeze,
Wrap up warm everyone, so we don't freeze.

Now it's summer with the hot sun,
The leaves have turned green,
They're filled with so much colour,
It's as if I'm in a dream.

It's gone chilly, we might all freeze,
The leaves have fallen off the tree,
Now the leaves are no more,
They all scattered on the floor.

### Sam Greenland (8)
Griffe Field Primary School, Derby

# Butterflies

Butterfly, butterfly, beautiful butterfly,
Flutter by, flutter by, beautiful butterfly.

Butterfly, butterfly, lands on a flower,
Flutters by, flutters by and drinks up the nectar.

Butterfly, butterfly, patterns on your wings,
Flutter by, flutter by, beautiful colours passing by.

Beautiful butterfly, butterfly flutters by.

**Katie Louise Birks (7)**
Griffe Field Primary School, Derby

# If I Could Ride A Giraffe To School

If I could ride a giraffe to school,
what would my friends say?
Wow! That's cool!
'Can we have a ride?
Can we have a ride?'
'OK, hang on a sec,
while I slide down her neck.
We can get on together,
come on we can climb its tail,'
with its head in the sky,
we would sit up high.
We could see houses and gardens,
she'd stop for a sec to have a snack,
but what would that be -
the leaves from trees!
When we get to school,
I'd say, 'Thank you,
and stay by the gate and wait!'

**Bridgette Chetwyn (7)**
Griffe Field Primary School, Derby

# The World

The world is where we live,
The world is full of life,
The world is a place where we can explore,
The world is a home for us and animals.
Wherever you go, the world is around you,
The world was once dark and empty,
Now there is light and it's busy.
The people have created new technology,
Like aeroplanes that help us reach other countries.
Each country has a different culture,
People have invented cars, phones, televisions and computers.
The world is wonderful!

**Nathaniel Kalyan (7)**
Griffe Field Primary School, Derby

# Mythical Dragons

Dragons spread their wings and hover in the sky,
Others stay and get ready to fly,
Some like to swirl and some like to twist,
Some never do this.
Eight were doing tricks and seven were doing sky kicks,
Four never joined in.

They were doing stunts and raced all around,
They were hunting for food, where could the animals be found?
There were big animals and small, there were even deadly animals too.
Creatures who fly and prowl on the ground . . .
Watch out – they're coming for you!

The animals ran away and sprinted to their homes,
The dragons had nothing to get, so they lost their treat,
If they went faster they would get some meat!

**Amelia Appleby (8)**
Griffe Field Primary School, Derby

# Football Poem!

I like football.
Liverpool are my favourite team,
I love to watch them play.
In the League, Sturridge scores
Every Saturday.
The captain, Stevie G.
Sterling score the goals!
Brendan Rogers, the Manager,
Saying, 'Come on Liverpool! Liverpool!'
And they score a goal!
*Bang, bang, bang!*
Liverpool say, 'Yes!'

**Taran Singh Hayre (8)**
Griffe Field Primary School, Derby

# War

Destructive bombs hit the attacked Earth,
surrounded by burning flames.

Shattered homes crumbled into crispy, black ash,
scattered remains of ruined lives.

The path of death crept along Liberia's back,
the city shook wildly.

Fear spread in the country,
the navy-blue sky faded into charcoal grey clouds of smoke.

Lots of shooting guns cut through the night.

**Simran Belleh (8)**
Griffe Field Primary School, Derby

# Stars

Dancing, shining, sparkling,
Lighting up the midnight sky,
Full of shapes playing,
Big Dipper,
Three Sister's
Making the night full of wonder
And not giving me
a fright at all.

**Lianna-Rose Shilton (7)**
Griffe Field Primary School, Derby

# Space Poem

My alien friend, Zog,
who comes from the planet, Mars,
said the glittering stars
are near to Mars.

The moon,
came out at noon,
what made Earth dark?
What made a spark?

Climb aboard my rocket ship,
on a journey to the stars.

Shooting stars,
flying to Mars,
hitting asteroids on the way.

My friend
went to Mars,
but he didn't like it,
because there were no cars.

**Samuel Burdis (8)**
Griffe Field Primary School, Derby

# Flowers

Roses are scarlet,
Asters are violet,
Buttercups are amber,
Bright, bold and beautiful they are.

Lilies are winter white,
Tulips are pretty pink,
Forget-me-nots are baby blue,
Swaying happily in the breeze.

Sunflowers are golden,
Pansies are maroon,
Orchids are turquoise,
Growing under the gigantic sun,
Bringing fun for everyone.

**Kiran Chohan (7)**
Griffe Field Primary School, Derby

# Some Sweets

Some sweets are sticky and
some sweets are icky.
Some sweets are yucky and
some sweets are mucky.
Some sweets you have to lick and
some sweets you eat off a stick.

But most of all
I love them all!

**Paige Lockley (8)**
Griffe Field Primary School, Derby

# Cars

Cars are brilliant in many ways,
so impressive how they can be
built in just a day.
To shape metal into a car,
wow!
Amazing I do say,
to choose from a variety of colours,
red, yellow, black, green or blue,
it's amazing.
From sports cars to super cars,
to hatchbacks to 4 x 4s.
There's so many to choose from,
so which one is yours?

**Aaron Gill (8)**
Griffe Field Primary School, Derby

# Sweets

Delicious, scrumptious and a delight,
sugary sweet, full of my type.
It's a very special treat,
really, very sweet, just for me and you
to share, try it if you dare.
All these fantastic sweets
are always everywhere.

**Hana Niaz Evans (7)**
Griffe Field Primary School, Derby

# Butterflies

B utterflies are colourful
U se the colours, it's wonderful
T hey are very nice
T hey also eat my rice
E arly, when the morning is past
R emember, the butterflies are quite fast
F ly to the butterflies in the sky
L ike you see up very high
I n the morning it's bright
E at when it's night
S o happy when you take flight.

**Sabrina Adam (8)**
Leicester International School, Leicester

# When I Met An Alien On Mars

S ome day I will go to Mars
P acing up and down, counting the stars
A n alien pops his head out of a crater
C edar was his name and he had a cheese grater
E ventually he commented with a remark that was snide

F our wriggling tentacles coming out of his side
A big, oval face, with a frown to break glass
C ommending himself, he said to a class
'T ruly I am of course the best
S omeday I will really go to Mars, but instead, on a search for a quest.'

**Madinah Ahmedjee (10)**
Leicester International School, Leicester

# Space Adventure

Maryam Is my name
The astronaut's game
I need a locket
To open a rocket
I always meet space
'Cos it is my favourite place
On the way to Mars
I saw a lot of stars
In the moon I feel gloomy
But I am glad that it is very roomy
I tried to smell the ground, but I just could not
When I looked up at the sun I remembered that it was hot
I saw a big rock on the moon
I dug and dug and found a silver spoon.

**Maryam Yusuf Jibhal (10)**
Leicester International School, Leicester


# Light

Light is bright
Light is at night
My kite is white
I like the kite
Light is from the sky
Clouds are beautiful and from the sky
Clouds are really high
Mummy is really nice.

**Sudais Saleh (8)**
Leicester International School, Leicester

# Rainbow

Rainbow in the sky,
It looks like colours can fly,
Rainbow, rainbow,
Red, orange, yellow, green and blue,
Rainbow, rainbow,
Red, orange, yellow, green and blue.

**Haarithaa Ali (8)**
Leicester International School, Leicester

# Colours

The world is full of colours
above, the sky is blue
the moonshine gave us light
the sun is yellow
this is a show
the grass is green. Wow!
The world has many colours
the flowers have many colours
big and small flowers
and so many secret colours
examples of green and red.

**Muhammad Imran Hassam (8)**
Leicester International School, Leicester

# Space Is Cool

I'm on Earth, gazing at the moon
thinking what I could do if I could zoom.
I'm in a rocket, closing the door, getting ready to soar,
I'm in space, in my rocket, getting sucked into a pocket.
I'm in a pocket, in my rocket, it's all because I didn't lock it,
I came out, I'm in a truck on a hot summer's day.
I'm on Mars and I can see stars
And it all happened today.

**Ibrahim Khalif (9)**
Leicester International School, Leicester

# The Live Planet

Blue as oceans
Green as grass
Bright in colours
Only planet that has life
More water
Less land
Still living
Still making
Still growing

What is it?

The Planet Earth.

**Ayesha Ahmed (10)**
Leicester International School, Leicester

# Space Dream

As my eyes open wide,
I realise I am no longer next to the tide,
I believe I am in space,
because there is no trace
of Earth and my house
and my little mouse.

All of a sudden it's bright,
I realise I am facing a light
and then I see the sun
and I start having fun.

As I see a star
I realise it is Mars
and as my eyelids droop down,
I want to go back to my home town
and as I open my eyes,
I realise I am next to the tide.

**Faheemah Sidat (10)**
Leicester International School, Leicester

# Space

I am in space,
Seeing aliens face-to-face,
I'm next to a star,
Where all the broken rockets are.
I'm looking at universal rings,
I don't need any more extra things,
I am being sucked by a black hole,
Now I am a helpless black mole.

**Hamza Rafi (9)**
Leicester International School, Leicester

# The Unknown World

There in space, lies big, small and medium balls
Which are planets
In the darkness a white cylinder goes by
Back of the white cylinder there is fire
Is it a white bird?
Is it an asteroid?
No, it's a rocket!
The astronauts say hi
Then the rocket splits
Apart, right by Venus
I wish I could go into the rocket and lock it
Suddenly the rocket shakes, like burning cakes
And takes off into unknown world
Where there are no planets.

**Mudassir Ahmad (8)**
Leicester International School, Leicester

# Space Is Cool

I'm on Earth, gazing at the moon,
Wondering what I could do if I zoom.
I'm in a rocket, thinking about what would be in pocket,
I'm staring at the moon in the camera's zoom.
I'm on Mars, eating some chocolate bars,
I'm on Venus, because I got the coolness.
But, I'm just on Earth with my family.

**Muhammad Sidat (9)**
Leicester International School, Leicester

# Space

S un shining on Earth
P urple astronauts falling from space
A mazing space on top of the world
C rying people when they get stuck
E ating cheese on the moon.

**Angel Katoch (8)**
Mellor Community Primary School, Leicester

# Space

S tars twinkling brightly in the dark night sky
P eople fly with rockets in the bright sky
A stronauts exploring space in their own dream
C haracters in books flying to space
E lves watching the space rocket launch at midnight.

**Matthew Godfree (8)**
Mellor Community Primary School, Leicester

# Space

S tars twinkling brightly at night-time
P lanets have been orbiting stars
A ll stars come out at night and twinkle
C ool planets are orbiting the stars
E ven though it is night-time light comes.

**Hena Hitesh (7)**
Mellor Community Primary School, Leicester

# Space

The powerful sun
roasting, bright white
marshmallows in space
the wonderful place
out of Earth and
the astronauts jumping
to Mars in the galaxy of space.

**Mu'aad Riyaz Ahmad Kadar (7)**
Mellor Community Primary School, Leicester

# Space

S tars twinkle in the dark, scary sky
P lanets are different from other, good, nice planets
A sun is a big, hot, fiery ball
C hildren must like to look at the stars and the moon
E veryone loves space!

**Nadia Ismael (8)**
Mellor Community Primary School, Leicester

# Space

S tars twinkling brightly at night-time
P lanets are round like golf balls
A ll stars come out when the sun goes in
C ircular planets, moons and suns are huge
E ven though night-time light comes.

**Colby Morrissey (8)**
Mellor Community Primary School, Leicester

# Space

S tars twinkling bright in the night
P lanets are in space
A stronauts go into space by a rocket
C hildren want to see Mars
E gypt is a hot country.

### Prashyam Dineshcha (8)
Mellor Community Primary School, Leicester


# Space

The burning, bright orange sun
exploding like a volcano
The powerful flames
protecting the fiery sun
The rocky moon is enormous.

### Mohammed Isa Iqbal (8)
Mellor Community Primary School, Leicester


# Space

S hooting stars like shiny, gold cars
P lanets close to the sun are really hot, like Mercury
A lovely moon doing its job, moving around the Earth
C ausing waves, the moon makes tides only
E veryone knows about planets, except babies.

### Shaun Singh Rehal (7)
Mellor Community Primary School, Leicester

# Space

The powerful sun, roasting
high and shining
bright like shining stars.
Roasting fluffy, white marshmallows,
silver stars crashing together
in dark space.

### Mya Mason (8)
Mellor Community Primary School, Leicester

# Space

S un, burning hot like fire
P lanets can be different sizes
A little bit of rock from the asteroid belts
C ool planets have colourful colours
E ven though we live on Earth, the universe is endless.

### Dhruvi Chudasama (8)
Mellor Community Primary School, Leicester

# Space

Burning brightly, like flames of fire
The fiery flames keep us warm
The planets sitting, looking at the stars
The planets flying near the galaxies.

### Deena Niran (8)
Mellor Community Primary School, Leicester

# Space

Burning, bright light, like lava spitting from an enormous volcano,
The first man to walk on the moon was Neil Armstrong,
The powerful, fiery flames burning on the hot sun,
Planets glow with warmth from the enormous sun.

**Georgia Ndigwa (8)**
Mellor Community Primary School, Leicester

# Space

S tars shining like shiny glitter
P lanets crashing
A stronauts floating around space
C hildren excited to go to space
E verything dark at night.

**Rohit Kaler (8)**
Mellor Community Primary School, Leicester

# Moon

A large moon appears at night,
There is a bright star in space.
An ugly alien lives in space,
A big rocket travels to space,
There are many planets in space.

**Francisca Macedo (9)**
Oaklands School, Leicester

# Moon

There is a scary alien on a planet,
An enormous rocket flies in the sky.
The hot sun is sweating,
The sparkling stars are dazzling.
The planets are enormous and shiny.

**Aftab Tariq (9)**
Oaklands School, Leicester

# The Bright Star

The bright star
is shining,
The star is lighting the sky,
it's beautiful.

**Jason Chauhan (10)**
Oaklands School, Leicester

# Moon

The moon is round
in the bright sky.
The stars are bright
in the sky.
Aliens are very happy
going to the moon.

**Erin Burton (9)**
Oaklands School, Leicester

# My Big Idea

My idea is as red as a freshly-picked rose,
It tastes like Scotch Bonnet
making my taste buds scream in agony.
The aroma of boiling chillies
makes your eyes water.
My idea looks like a masterpiece,
waiting to be revealed.
It sounds like a baby wailing
for its dinner.
My idea feels like kneaded dough,
ready to bloom into bread.

**Aidan Hawkins (10)**
Olympic Primary School, Wellingborough

# A Bright Idea

My idea is as red as a beautiful rose,
It tastes like strawberry bubblegum melting in my mouth,
It smells like strawberries ripening as the summer breeze passes by,
It looks like red-hot peppers dancing on a parade, waiting to be
eaten,
It sounds like the air is whispering to me,
It feels like the heatwave is brushing against my face.

**Mia Olivia Plummer (11)**
Olympic Primary School, Wellingborough

# The Bright Idea

The idea came as a multicoloured rainbow, appearing out of nowhere,
It changes colour every two minutes.
I hope it doesn't bounce out of my head, like balls running around a street,
It comes at me, step by step as I walk around my room.
Now and then it opens, like a flower sprouting out of the ground,
Waiting for the idea to dance again.
I hope my friend had it too,
It tastes like a volcano!
It floats around in the air,
Feeling it is a sun coming towards me, turning me into a bright blue star.
It smells like all the delicious fruit mixed together into a fruit salad,
It sounds like a melody of music playing in my head.
If there are no ideas, there is no life . . .

**Ellie Daun (11)**
Olympic Primary School, Wellingborough

# My Idea

I have a stupendous idea,
It stretches elegantly to the far reaches of my mind . . .
*Bang!*
It's gone, for a long period of time and I suddenly begin to feel
slightly blind.

Unravelling, it's back for certain, (I think), but more mighty and
muscular,
But now I am stumbling around,
Eyes tingling, fingers searching,
I collapse dramatically to the tender ground.

Eventually I can visualise again,
But the breathtaking suggestion had vanished, it's gone -
I stand, motionless, stationary, absent-minded,
While it perches sniggering, in the corner, whispering,
'I'm back, I'm back, but not for long!'

I had a stupendous idea,
But now it does not exist, it's gone,
If only I had jotted it down . . . !

**Renée Pierre-White (11)**
Olympic Primary School, Wellingborough

# The Moon

Anlmal-seeker
Light-killer
Peace-bringer
Dark-lover
Gravity-offender
Night-owner
Earth-protector
Sweet-dreamers
Darkness-fighter

The moon!

**Paige White (10)**
Olympic Primary School, Wellingborough

# The Sun

It brings light,
It brings life.
It makes the birds sing,
It gets you up in the morning.
It helps plants grow,
It brings . . . hope.

It is the sun.

**Ellis Gavin Bigg (10)**
Olympic Primary School, Wellingborough

# Shooting Star

An angel falls,
She begins to stall,
A heavenly cry up above,
She's so beautiful, like a dove.

It burns like fire from the underworld,
But it is bright blue – from Heaven above,
If I could catch it
I would give it to my mum to show my love.

The shooting star,
It's just too far,
Not touchable with my bare hands,
Only if it landed upon the smooth warming sands.

**Andrew Kane (10)**
Olympic Primary School, Wellingborough

# Spectacular Space

S  pectacular stars shining bright
P  lanet Pluto gets destroyed
A  n amazing time portal to discover
C  aptured asteroid, just in time
E  xciting adventures have been explored.

**Tachelle Oddy (9)**
Olympic Primary School, Wellingborough

# Politics!

David Cameron,
He is the Conservative's leader,
He is the money believer,
Don't vote for Labour.

Nigel Farage,
The UKIP leader,
He is a money-needer,
He has a Lamborghini in his garage.

Ed Milliband,
The Labour leader,
He has a disco fever,
He lives in Labour Land.

Nicola Sturgeon,
The SNP leader,
She is the Scottish money-feeder,
The Scottish surgeon.

The Green party,
Love the colour green,
The Green Machine,
They are a bit barky.

**Harley Tomkins (10)**
Olympic Primary School, Wellingborough

**85**

# My Dolly Dog

My Dolly Dog,
tinier
than her brother,
tinier
than her mother.
She is my Dolly Dog.
The brown on her looks like
a brown chick's feathers
and a hard nut.
Some of her is as black as soot
from a fire.

**Lacey Marie Bailey (9)**
Olympic Primary School, Wellingborough


# Sweets!

The thought of sweets is so divine,
It makes me wish
They were all mine!

From Rowntree's Randoms
To Swizzles Refreshers,
I want them all,
His, his and hers.

Sweets are the foremost in my mind,
They're better than the rest,
I wish I had a sufficient amount,
That the mountain was as almighty as my chest.

**Daniel Pearman (10)**
Olympic Primary School, Wellingborough

# My Idea

I have a brilliant idea,
It's like an explosion coming out of my ear,
Lots of spewing fireworks spinning furiously,
Like a wild tornado around my exhausted brain,
Then – It vanished into the flowing fresh air,
I'm searching vigorously,
Bursting like dynamite to find it,
Before my brain overloads!

### Kani Pierre-White (11)
Olympic Primary School, Wellingborough

# Space Mysteries

S olar systems everywhere
P umping planets, like Earth
A mazing sights to behold
C limbing on asteroids
E normous worlds to see

Space and time may riddle
Your mind, but stars won't
Space and mysteries that are unsolved
But two planets with life
Now just one.

### Ben Charter (9)
Olympic Primary School, Wellingborough

# I Saw

I saw the moon sweeping across the sky,
I saw the sun next to it,
So bright,
So long, farewell,
I don't want to leave this pretty sight!
What shall I do?
I don't want to leave this planet,
I've got an idea,
I'm going to the moon,
So I can live there for ever.

**Paige Gilbey (9)**
Olympic Primary School, Wellingborough

# Space

S wiftly, the stars shimmer
P eacefully, planets are harmonious
A stonishingly, shooting stars glide across the sky
C ontinuously, the planets spin
E xcitedly, the planets spin.

**Ann-Jonai Finletter (9)**
Olympic Primary School, Wellingborough

# Space

S parkling stars in the sky
P eacefully the planets move
A stronauts fly around space
C alm planets float around
E xtraordinary shapes of the planets.

**Mia Annie-May Boston (9)**
Olympic Primary School, Wellingborough

# Haiku About Space

Space is amazing,
Space is very shimmering,
Space is fabulous.

### Miller Dufty (9)
Olympic Primary School, Wellingborough

# Space

S hooting stars next to Mars
P eaceful planets in harmony
A liens live in harmony
C annot breathe in space's atmosphere
E nd of the trip to wonderful space.

### Preston Stewart-Clark (8)
Olympic Primary School, Wellingborough

# Space

S tars shimmer in the night sky
P assing rockets zoom by
A liens on Mars
C omets whizz past
E arth is in the galaxy.

### Chloe Carter (8)
Olympic Primary School, Wellingborough

# Space

M ars is all red
A re they dangerous or nice?
R eady to launch, ready to fly and head for Mars
S tars, all high stars are bright red to grant a wish tonight.

### Serena Georgina Locke (7)
Olympic Primary School, Wellingborough

# Space

Space, space, a wonderful place
Mercury, Venus, Earth and Mars live high above the stars
Watch the comets as they tear all over the place
Astronauts having a rocket race
There is nothing better than space.

**Dominic Edward White (8)**
Olympic Primary School, Wellingborough

# Space

The nine planets.
Mercury, Venus, Earth, Uranus
Mars, Jupiter, Saturn,
Neptune, Pluto,
Orbit around the gas sun.

**Jack Fitch (8)**
Olympic Primary School, Wellingborough

# What Am I?

Darkness-bringer
Star-shimmerer
Planet-collector
Astronaut-seeker
Rocket-hider
Going to bed-maker
Moonlight-finder
Pluto-destroyer
Land-discoverer
Solar system-controller.

What am I?

Space!

**Grace Cooper (8)**
Olympic Primary School, Wellingborough

# Up To The Sky

Leaving Earth was like leaving home for ever,
When I go to space it was blacker than sun,
Seeing the shining, spectacular sun,
I move out of the solar system
It felt as if the solar system was watching me.
Leaving the Milky Way is like a spiral out of control,
Seeing a nebula cloud is an emerald flying around.
Bouncing out of the giant, gorgeous galaxy,
Watching an asteroid is like an onion ring.
Not ever going home, ever,
Because of how it made me feel.

**Scott Perry (10)**
Sherwood Junior School, Mansfield

# The Lottie Planet

The trees are giraffe necks,
Air is a hot chocolate waiting for me,
Mountain peaks are pencils that scrape the cloud,
Cheetahs sprint like Usain Bolt,
Volcanoes are constantly being sick,
Dirty, dark, dismal caves loom in the distance,
Rivers flow like golden corn,
Dogs bark like wolves screaming,
Birds fly like aeroplanes,
Grass is a great, green, gorgeous emerald,
Dolphins are water acrobats,
Sea waves are showers.
The planet is a weird, wonderful place,
Sky is a blue, black blanket that acts like a roof,
People stroll around like nothing has happened.

**Charlotte Jones-Duncalf (10)**
Sherwood Junior School, Mansfield

# Space

Leaving Earth is like giving up my family,
Staring at the sparkling sun is staring at a loved one.
The splendid solar system was waving goodbye,
I'm leaving my greatest treasure behind.
Viewing a nebula cloud made me realise that space is an
outstanding location,
Abandoning the galaxy, notice how much I need it.
Black holes are talking as humans,
I noticed an asteroid belt, like a hundred floating diamonds.

**Electra Shelby Lowe (10)**
Sherwood Junior School, Mansfield


# Flying Up In Space

When I'm leaving Earth,
It looks as tiny as a mouse.

The blackness is a bottomless pit,
I'm suddenly moving out of this busy solar system.

Shimmering and shining is the sun in the distance,
Stepping out of the Milky Way is like a rainbow dying off.

Floating up, I see a nebula cloud as fluffy as cotton,
Whilst I'm flying, I see a sly black hole that tried to suck me in.

A luminous, large asteroid belt went by,
I love it here in space.

I'm never going back,
It's as if I'm in a dream, as beautiful as a precious gem.

**Ruby Collier (10)**
Sherwood Junior School, Mansfield

# Travelling Through Space!

Leaving Earth is like leaving all my treasures,
going into an unknown world.
Going up and above, into space, seeing wishes come true,
seeing a giant fireball burn
is as if I can see a happy fire.
I move out of the solar system,
seeing gorgeous gems cast over a black blanket.
Leaving the Milky Way is like kissing goodbye
to my favourite chocolate bar.
Oh! But seeing the pink candyfloss floating away,
it puts a smile on my face.
Oh no! It's time to go,
time to put my feet on my humble home.

**Evie Steed (10)**
Sherwood Junior School, Mansfield

# Up In Space

Earth is like a tiny dot as my rocket soars up high,
Space is a dark corridor with stars,
The spectacular, shimmering sun shines over Earth,
As I leave the solar system sad planets wave goodbye,
The Milky Way looks like a huge, bright spiral,
Nebula clouds are colourful dust decorating the darkness,
A giant, glorious galaxy starts to disappear,
An angry black hole is snatching stars from the sky,
Asteroid belts look like rocks on the beaches,
Space is so wonderful, I'm never going back home!

**Lia Mae Fowler (9)**
Sherwood Junior School, Mansfield

# Space!

Leaving Earth is strange, the planets are lovely,
Planets are like walking on Pot Noodles, crunching, crunching,
crunching.
Mars is like a chocolate bar,
It is as brown as mud.
Black holes are very dark, you can't walk in them,
because there is no powerful gravity to pull you down.
Two planets are just ice and water,
They glisten like a diamond, reflecting light.

**Carly Hartshorn (10)**
Sherwood Junior School, Mansfield

# The Galaxy

Leaving friendly Earth is like starting a new life,
floating through space is a dream come true.
The sparkling sun shines down on homely Earth,
the rusty spaceship sprinted out of the solar system.
Leaving the Milky Way is like being praised by God,
Nebula clouds are very exciting because of all the vibrant colours.
Rapidly racing through the galaxy,
black holes are mouths that suck in your soul.
Zooming past asteroid belts is like tennis balls coming at your face,
but, when you think you're not going home . . .
It's all different!

**Benjamin Neil Clay (10)**
Sherwood Junior School, Mansfield

## Six Ways To Look At The Sun

The sun is like an erupting volcano ready to explode
Sun hides behind the moon and does not come out
Sun, why are you so bright?
The sun wished he could be left alone in space!
Sun talks,
The golden sun lies in the starry sky waiting to be revealed.

**Lily Jane Fletcher (10)**
Sherwood Junior School, Mansfield

## The Unknown Planet

Trees are like Cheese Strings,
The air is the only oxygen I breathe,
Mouldy mountains I can see,
Animals I can greet.
Birds are laughing,
Clouds are like fluffy mash,
The sky is a blue blanket,
Green grass you can play on.
The sea is waving hello,
Rivers are like a big surprise,
Caves are a never-ending hole,
Cute cats are pouncing playfully,
Dogs are walking,
Unicorns are like butterflies.

**Isabella MacDonald (10)**
Sherwood Junior School, Mansfield

**95**

# My Own Planet

The trees are like a wizard
The air is like a thin crisp
The mountains are like a knife
The animals are so like a baby
The birds are beautiful, like a rose
The clouds are like candy
The sky is like a cave
The grass is like gas
The sea is a sheet of blue
The river is like a bluebell
The caves are like a black hole
The volcano spits sweets
The fish are slippery fellows
The bear is fierce.

**Kieran Sime (10)**
Sherwood Junior School, Mansfield

# Out Of This World

When I close my eyes I think of space
The zooming rockets of all colours and kinds
Strange aliens pop up, saying, 'Hello!'
Beautiful meteors coming from every direction.
All the shimmering stars up above my head,
But best of all the blazing sun shines on me.

**Ellie Cutts (9)**
Sherwood Junior School, Mansfield

# Space

Space Is a wonderful thing
there's a whole bunch of things in space
The colourful planets
rockets zooming up into space
Glimmering stars reflecting orange planets
aliens flew from their planet
hoping to find something nice
The dusty moon filled with astronauts
floating in the sky
What a sight it was
seeing the tiny astronauts
and then the burning hot sun appear.

**Harry George French (9)**
Sherwood Junior School, Mansfield

# Space

Space is a wonderful place
with twinkling stars and zooming comets.
The dark sky is a black hole,
astronauts floating in the air,
rockets whizzing around the atmosphere.
The blinding sun is as bright as a flaming fire,
all moons are in position,
the solar system is spinning around.
Aliens will come and meet you,
gravity is not strong enough anymore.
Is space a place for you?

**Mia Archer (9)**
Sherwood Junior School, Mansfield

# Space

Stars, stars
Planets and stars
I can see Jupiter
I can see Mars.
Blasting rockets
Fly through the sky
Passing round cheese
and shining stars.
Wonderful, amazing
and so much more.
Aliens talking babble,
astronauts floating off.

**Nancy Kirk (9)**
Sherwood Junior School, Mansfield

# The Sun

The sun is a burning skyscraper
lighting up the darkness.
The sun is a phoenix head
peering over the land.
The sun is a glittering pound coin
shining above the clouds.
The sun is a burning, bright orange
flames lighting up the land.
The sun is a lion
sleeping on the clouds.
the sun says,
'Today is bright.'

**Taryn Dennis (10) & Emily**
Sherwood Junior School, Mansfield

# Space

The astronauts, going to space, 3, 2, 1, blast-off!
The rocket takes off and reaches the atmosphere
and arrives in space.

The moon, made of cheese, with cows jumping over it,
at the speed of light,
the rocket takes off to Mars.

Mars, very hot, like fire,
volcanoes ready to rumble and explode,
mysterious creatures lurking around the scorching hot planet.
Now let's set off for Saturn.

Saturn's rings spinning around like the fastest things,
the shiny Saturn rings like wheels.
Now to Pluto,
Pluto, thought to be a planet, but actually a dwarf planet,
the smallest of them all and tiny.

Many other galaxies yet to explore,
bright like the sun everywhere in space.

**Harry Aaron John Cooper (9)**
Sherwood Junior School, Mansfield

# The Galaxy

The galaxy is an explosion of colours above the dusty sea,
The sun is like a derelict building, left getting worse and worse,
Comets are fireballs that Zeus dropped,
Mars is a volcanic rock that is ready to go *boom!*
Meteors scrape through the face of the Earth,
The people fly and say goodbye.

**Henry Simpson (10)**
Sherwood Junior School, Mansfield

# The Galaxy

The galaxy is Pegasus' crystal wings about to fly off,
The galaxy is the Empire State Building's gleaming glass windows,
The galaxy says, 'I'm covered in sparkles.'
The galaxy is like a colourful, curled snake,
The galaxy is Zeus' powerful lightning,
The galaxy is a clash of colours about to explode.

**McCallum Johnson & Kayleigh Jo Clark (10)**
Sherwood Junior School, Mansfield

# The Milky Way

The Milky Way is a towering skyscraper,
The Milky Way is like a glittering horde of stars,
do not dare to touch or you're going to turn to a diamond,
staring down at the Minotaur's muscles.
The Milky Way is a diamond blanket, looking down on Earth,
The Milky Way is a deck of cards, falling down like it's the end.
The Milky Way is a world of diamonds
looking down on the Cyclops' eye.
The Milky Way is a rainbow of colours,
The Milky Way says, 'Goodnight World.'
The Milky Way stares down at the solar system.

**Devon Wheatley (10)**
Sherwood Junior School, Mansfield

# Stars

A star is a glimmer ot gold in the galaxy
A star is a genie in a lamp, casting wish upon wish
A star is a galactic space bubble
A star is a thing that holds your loved ones
A star is a wish-caster above, where no one can see.

**Mitchell Folwell (9)**
Sherwood Junior School, Mansfield

# Six Ways To Look At The Galaxy

The galaxy is an art gallery, filled with splashes of colour
and painting, like an original by Pablo Picasso.
The galaxy is Pegasus' wings stretching wide
to soar into the darkness.

The galaxy is Hercules' muscles, always powerful,
always big and will never break.
The galaxy is a kaleidoscope of colours,
shattering snapping, fracturing like glass.

The galaxy is a cat's eye,
swirling into a pool of darkness.
The galaxy says,
'Every day I'm up at sunrise
with the breeze in my face and the sparkling sky.'

**Alyssa State (10)**
Sherwood Junior School, Mansfield

# The Solar Eclipse

The solar eclipse is a deep mine
bringing darkness when it is supposed to be light.
The solar eclipse is a fiery dragon
with its breath extinguished.
The solar eclipse says,
'I am going to take a rest from shining.'
The solar eclipse is a firefly
whose fuse just went out.
The solar eclipse is Zeus
blocking the sun with his powers.
The solar eclipse is a violent, fiery, red coat
with a mysterious black lining.

**Corey Ian Lee Widdowson (10)**
Sherwood Junior School, Mansfield

# Six Ways Of Looking At Saturn

Saturn is like a married planet, its ring is a wedding band,
Saturn's ring is like people surrounding a shop,
Saturn's ring is the London Eye spinning around in circles,
Saturn is a shining diamond floating in the sky,
Saturn is strong, like Hercules,
Saturn says, 'Tonight will be a good night.'

**Carl Hicken (10)**
Sherwood Junior School, Mansfield

# Mercury

Mercury Is lIke an angry volcano
Don't get too near, otherwise you're toast!
Mercury, why are you so hot?
Mercury wishes she wasn't so hot
Mercury toasts the solar system
Mercury makes the cheesy moon melt like on a fierce grill.

**Kelsey Sills-Kemp & Alana Mollatt (10)**
Sherwood Junior School, Mansfield

# A Batron

Caves are gloomy, creepy and deserted,
animals are like us roaming the Earth.
Clouds are dark and misty,
trees are stumps.
Flowers don't grow,
the sun is rotten.
Waves are sea monsters,
grass is brown and rotten.
The sky is dark and terrifying,
Mountains are faces in the night.
Mist is a ghost creeping up on us.

**Katie May (10)**
Sherwood Junior School, Mansfield

# Out Of This World

The sparkling stars cover the sky
and the moon is so bright and looms
The rockets are speeding like a jet
it is pitch-black.
These are the beautiful planets,
Mercury, Venus, Earth, Mars, Jupiter, Saturn,
Uranus, Neptune, Pluto and the moon and sun.
The sun is like glitter
meteors make massive craters.
There are different colours and comets
you may see some astronauts.

**Liam Slaney (9)**
Sherwood Junior School, Mansfield

# Saturn

Saturn's ring is like a circle of life,
Saturn's ring is a band waiting to be put on a finger,
Saturn's ring is a prized possession.

**Bradley Dennis (10)**
Sherwood Junior School, Mansfield

# Earth

Flashing
Awesome and great
Swirling around the sun
Unique and special, it's blessed
The Earth.

**Samantha Agboghidi (10)**
Sycamore Academy, Nottingham

# Moons, Rockets And Stars

S hootlng my rocket to the moon.
P lace called the sun that is burning hot and you die.
A nd I see shooting stars.
C an we explore the moon?
E xplore the moon? That is fine, let's go!

### Harrison Marritt (9)
Sycamore Academy, Nottingham

# Outstanding Planets

S himmering
H armful Venus is as beautiful as space
O utstanding planets
O ut of this world
T errific Jupiter
I mpressive
N ice place
G igantic Jupiter

S hining space
T winkling stars
A tmosphere
R ed Mars.

### Yaldah Sajad (9)
Sycamore Academy, Nottingham

# Space

S pectacular stars shining brightly.
P lanets glitter like bright stars in the blue sky.
A ir helps humans breathe.
C an always be hot and boiling.
E arth is a peaceful planet.

### Hu Jie Wang (9)
Sycamore Academy, Nottingham

# Planets

P eacefully, the stars combine together as a big family.
L ively, the planets stand together as one.
A ir helps humans breathe.
N eptune is colder than the Antarctica.
E arth is a peaceful planet.
T he sun's temperature is very hot.

**Hassan Kahiye (9)**
Sycamore Academy, Nottingham

# Stars

S pectacular star in the twilight sky.
T errific to see shooting stars.
A mazing as the stars combine as a family.
R ocket speed.
S cientific stars.

**Hamza Kahiyye (9)**
Sycamore Academy, Nottingham

# Stardust And Moon Rocks

G ust of lightning hits the Earth with unbelievable power.
A lien UFOs race like the speed of light across the face of the Earth.
L ike a hurricane, the sun burst into gleaming flames.
A mazing stars orbit around the Earth.
e X tra stars shining in the bright sky.
Y ou're amazing, bright star.

**Damari Barnes (9)**
Sycamore Academy, Nottingham

# Starlight Acrostic Poem

S himmering stars
T empting to reach up and touch
A mazing
R euniting
L ights up the world
I ncreasing the light
G lows in the darkness
H ope beholds light
T ruly blessed.

**Eliavah Abrahams (9)**
Sycamore Academy, Nottingham

# Kaboom

Starlight
Come to the moon
Enjoy the moonlight sky
Unseen shooting star comes
Your way.

**Mukhtar Oyeleke (9)**
Sycamore Academy, Nottingham

# Star

S himmering in the space, a group of stars are coming together to make a sun.
T ogether all the stars are combining as a family.
A mazingly, the planets are surrounding the sun and making a solar system.
R apidly a shooting star launches down, going to hit Earth.

**Grace Mesa (8)**
Sycamore Academy, Nottingham

YoungWriters

# The Universe

S hining stars
H armful Venus
O pportunity to see beautifulness
O utstanding
T alented twinkling stars
I maginative
N ice place
G alaxy

S himmering moon
T errific Jupiter
A tmosphere
R ed Mars
S hooting stars.

**Jazmin Lee (9)**
Sycamore Academy, Nottingham

# Space Poem

Out of my window I can see
A comet which is going to shoot into the moon
And will make a dusty hole
Which will swoop dust over your eyes
Swirly Milky Way like some milk tornado
Stars like gold and silver coins
A double, double, double tornado
Like a cream egg has a splodge of swirly orange paint
A fiery bolt ball crashing to the Earth's crust!

**Wiktoria Godlewska (8)**
Sycamore Academy, Nottingham

# Untitled

Out of my blasting window, I see a galaxy and an asteroid fused together creating a mass destruction and the galaxy was annihilated.
Out of my super-charged swirling vortex, I see a satellite and a meteor shower destroys the satellite.
I see a trail behind the meteor creating a colourful, blazing, bluish brush.
The swirling vortex is about to teleport you to a magical land.
I see an exploding satellite with asteroids smashing and bashing the destroyed satellite.
Out of my special window, I see a solar system with one planet orbiting the other way round.

**Antonio Lewis (7)**
Sycamore Academy, Nottingham

# What I Can See

The shooting, sparkling stars in space
Look like a sparkling blue ball with glitter on it
And shooting through full black space
And through the pretty, clean windows.
I can see beautiful yellow stars.
Venus looks like a big chocolate ball.
Saturn looks like dough with a ring around it.
Jupiter looks like an orange cream ball with a cream colour with a little black.
The galaxy looks like lots of colour together.
Mars looks like a red and orange ball.
The Milky Way looks like a blurry colour altogether.
I can see a satellite flying through space.

**Mary Angel Tavares Gomes (8)**
Sycamore Academy, Nottingham

# Space

Out of my window I can see shooting stars that shine like the sun.
Venus is a big red paintball and it is so hot and warm like a teddy bear.
Mars is so round like Maltesers because it is round.
Earth has snowy ice-caps and has water clouds that swirl around fast.

**Asia Benjamin (7)**
Sycamore Academy, Nottingham

# Looking Out Of The Window

Out of the rocket window,
I can see an asteroid like a bursting paintball zooming past me.
I can see Earth coming towards me like a shooting star.
I can see a comet rushing past me like a twirling tornado.
I can see the Milky Way, it's like a collection of tiny people dancing.
I can see the stars like the sun.

**Jaiden Rio Hands (7)**
Sycamore Academy, Nottingham

# Space

Out of the window of my rocket,
I can see Mars that looks like a melting orange.
Venus looks like a Creme Egg
That explodes like a ball.
Out of the window I can see a vacuum.
Out of the window I can see
Shooting stars that shine like the sun.
Out of my window I can see
A beautiful galaxy.
Dun, dun, dun!

**Elteja Kvaukaite (8)**
Sycamore Academy, Nottingham

# In Space Alone 3

Out of the window I see
The asteroids swirling like a volcano.
A comet crashing to Venus.
I only hear silence.
I only see the moon crumbling apart
Like a twister that can break anything in its way.
Asteroids crashing like paintballs.
The Milky Way spinning like ultimate dust.
The sun's gas is boiling.
The fire boiling lava evacuating like ash.
Twirling like molten liquid tumbling down.
The gas, so hot it has millions of cans of Coke.

**Mohamed Amin Abdi (7)**
Sycamore Academy, Nottingham

# The Planets

Mercury is like a huge metal ball,
And it is the smallest of them all.
Venus got its things burnt off,
Because the sun gave a cough.

Now for the place we live on,
In a few billion years, bet it'll be gone.
It is black and green like flowers,
Sweet as April showers.

Mars is famous for its massive mountains,
And they shoot out fountains.
It is as red as blood,
Would you live there? I don't think I could.

**Eddie Patchett (9)**
Warren Hills Primary School, Coalville

# Whirlpool Wonder

I got in a spaceship,
I did,
To find a new discovery.

I've searched far and wide,
To search for things that hide.

I saw a mysterious thing,
That shines like,
Rubies and emeralds.

But when I touched the thing,
It made a sound like a ding,
Then I was deceived.

And I was sucked in!
And I discovered a thing,
Called a . . .
Space whirl pool!

I saw a mysterious creature,
It jumped on me,
I screamed, 'Argh!'

But I woke up,
But I found out,
It was just a dream . . .

**Jasmin Insley (9)**
Warren Hills Primary School, Coalville

# Galaxy Of The Unknown!

There was a galaxy,
And the planets were different types of balls for sport.
It was a magical place,
And on one planet aliens thought how to build a fort.

Then the black hole disappeared,
And then I was all alone.
The place looked crazy,
And the aliens wore ice cream cones!

I went to one planet,
And there was another black hole.
It led to the inside of the planet,
And it looked as dark as coal.

Then I went through,
And there was an alien named Blib-Blob.
He was scary,
And so was his friend, Flip-Flop.

They sold strange things like
Human eyes.
And human legs,
And they held onto them as tight as a kid with a kite.

I used to like aliens,
But now I realise they're just pests.

**Haylie Green (9)**
Warren Hills Primary School, Coalville

# Once I Met An Alien

Once I met an alien,
His name was Bose and he was gross.
We went through a hole,
Thinking it was owned by a mole.
But then we realised
That there was no rocket coming out of our pockets.
Bose wasn't actually gross, he was cool I suppose,
We saw a loon on Jupiter's moon.
Bose was jolly and his alien friend is called Holly.
We saw a man,
He looked like a blobby, blue, belly-flopping ball.
He was Balistic-Bob.
He had no friends but guess what?
He wore glasses,
But they had no lenses.

**Alice Smith (9)**
Warren Hills Primary School, Coalville

# Warren Hills In Space

Warren Hills went to space
Warren Hills' children are so excited
Warren Hills saw a meteorite
Warren Hills' children wish they were on the ground.

Warren Hills saw aliens
Warren Hills' children are so scared
Warren Hills' children wanted to go to the moon
They are now so excited just like before.

Warren Hills saw a colourful spaceship
Warren Hills was so amazed
Warren Hills' children wanted to have a ride
But Warren Hills' teacher said no!

**Chloe Kendrick (9)**
Warren Hills Primary School, Coalville

# Meeting An Alien!

Aliens are nice,
Aliens are good,
Aliens are horrid,
Will they suck my blood?

Will they eat me up?
Will they bake me in a pie?
Will they be nice?
Or will they make me cry?

Can they be freaky?
Can they be sticky?
Can they be creepy?
Or will they be slippy?

Do they have a ship?
Do they have a monster?
Will they feed me to the monster
Or hurt me with a lobster?

I wish they will be nice,
I wish they won't be horrid,
I hope I will be all right,
So I can eat my porridge.

So Aliens can be nice,
Aliens can be good,
Aliens can be horrid,
But will they suck my blood?

**Ashlee Cliff (9)**
Warren Hills Primary School, Coalville

# Things About Space

Rockets so colourful,
Rockets so beautiful.

The moon so rocky,
The moon so vast.

Aliens so slimy,
Aliens so climby.

Planets so fast,
Planets so slow.

The sun so bright,
The sun so tight.

Space so gloomy,
Space so dazzling.

**Katie Appleton (9)**
Warren Hills Primary School, Coalville

# Aliens In Space

Aliens, aliens in space
Aliens, aliens eating in space
Aliens as creepy as the dark black night
Aliens that you might like
Aliens, aliens with dark black eyes
Like a big meteorite
Aliens, aliens with slimy bodies.

**Tia Burton (9)**
Warren Hills Primary School, Coalville

# Meeting Aliens

Aliens are awesome
Aliens are scary
Aliens are creepy
And some are hairy.

Aliens are amazing
Aliens are strong
Aliens are terrified
And some are long.

Aliens are lazy
Aliens are massive
Aliens are bad
And some are hairy.

Aliens are funky
Aliens with smiles
Aliens are smiley
Two hungry crocodiles.

**Kevin Ulanowski (9)**
Warren Hills Primary School, Coalville

# Aliens

Aliens, aliens, freaky, skinny.
Aliens, aliens, spooky, creepy.
Never freak then they
Won't creep when you sneak.

**Jade Ford (10)**
Warren Hills Primary School, Coalville

# Aliens Are Dumb!

Aliens are dumb and aliens are slimy as snails.
Aliens smell and aliens have slimy heads.
Aliens with slimy arms and big eyes.
Aliens are weird, aliens are gruesome, aliens are super cool.
Aliens are strange and strong.
Aliens with super claws.

**Hasan Taslioglu (8)**
Warren Hills Primary School, Coalville

# I Hate Space

I hate space, it is boring
There is nobody there and there's no air
A planet is pretty cool but it still doesn't rule
So you think it's cool, well it drools
What if you got sucked into a black hole
In the hole, you will lose your soul
The people use you as a tool
Just so they can make you look like a fool
So you dive for a stick on a moon!

**Phillip Gez Wilks (10)**
Warren Hills Primary School, Coalville

# Mission: Mars

One day I went to space,
To planet Mars,
In a rocket ship,
Through the stars

When I got there after a few years,
Aliens I saw,
They had ray guns, it was scary,
They had a god called Core.

They put me in a cage,
To escape I KO'd the guard and grabbed
His key,
His name was Lee.

'Lee, you're coming with me.'
Then I sprinted for my shuttle,
But I kept dropping him,
'Lee, why are you so heavy?'

I picked up some alien money,
I made it to my shuttle,
By the time I got home,
Me and Lee were friends.

I had a daughter,
Called her Mindy,
The aliens had a plan to slaughter.

**Ethan Fortuin (10)**
Warren Hills Primary School, Coalville

# The Alien Poem

Aliens are awesome,
Aliens are fools,
Aliens are cool,
And they are small.

Aliens are special,
Aliens are cruel,
Aliens are spooky,
And they are vast.

Aliens are creepy,
Aliens are scary,
Aliens are sneaky,
And they are giant.

The time goes fast,
The time goes slow.

Aliens are bloody,
Aliens are gloomy,
Aliens are so dim,
This poem might carry on . . .

**Ilona Marek (9)**
Warren Hills Primary School, Coalville

# The Galaxy In Space

Galaxy In space
Aliens in space
Lollipop in space
Air in space
Explore space.

### Tiegan Parry (9)
Warren Hills Primary School, Coalville

# Children Meeting Aliens In Space!

Two children in space.
Two children have quite a paste.
Two children have quite a waste.
Two children had been in space.
Two children saw aliens.
Two children were shady.
Two children are friends with aliens.
Two children miss their friends.
Two children have schools.
Two children miss their mums.

### Demi Leigh King (9)
Warren Hills Primary School, Coalville

# The Beautiful Whirlpool

In space there is a whirlpool.
The whirlpool has lots of sparkles.
And the sparkles look like diamonds in the sky.
In the whirlpool the sparkles look like stars in the night sky.
In space, spacemen stare at the beautiful whirlpool
Like it's a space lady!
In space the whirlpool tricks the spacemen.

**Mia Efford (9)**
Warren Hills Primary School, Coalville

# Space

Stars twinkle
Spaceships fly
Meteors go boom
Gravity floats
Earth people
Sunshine
Moon cheese
Aliens – ugly
Solar system – colossal
Colours – adventurous
Pluto – tiny
Jupiter – big
Milky Way – epic
Mars – red
Pluto – blue
Earth – amazing.

**Cian-Rhys Waterman (8)**
Western Primary School, Grimsby

# Space Poem

Stars shining
Spaceship flying
Meteors zooming
Gravity floats
Earth people
Colours – bright
Sun-maker
Aliens – ugly
Milky Way – colossal
Moon craters
Planets – colourful
Rocket – fast
Solar system – giant
Craters – tiny.

**Martyne Dodd (9)**
Western Primary School, Grimsby

# Space

Stars twinkle
Spaceships fly
Meteors crash
Gravity floats
Earth – home
Pluto – tiny
Sun – fiery.

**Ellie Mae Lamberton (9)**
Western Primary School, Grimsby

# Space Kennings

Stars twinkling
Spaceship take-off
Meteors crashing
Gravity floating
Earth – alive
Milky Way – massive
Moon shining
Colours – brilliant
Sun – gassy
Solar system – colourful
Planets moving
Crater hole
Satellite turning
Comet falling
Alien – grimy.

**Noah Langley (9)**
Western Primary School, Grimsby

# Space Poem

Stars shine
Spaceships fly
Meteors boom
Gravity – none
Earth – home
Planets – home
Moon – big
Alien colours
Sun – bright
Pluto – tiny
Rocket – huge
Rocket – tiny.

**Connor Martin (9)**
Western Primary School, Grimsby

# Space Kennings Poem

Stars gleaming
Spaceships flying
Meteors floating
Gravity-holding
Earth-living
Milky Way – colourful
Aliens – gooey
Craters – big
Moon – bumpy
Pluto – tiny
Planets – Mars
Colours – bright
Solar system – enormous
Space infinity
Venus – orange.

**Kira-Leigh Maynard Lewis (9)**
Western Primary School, Grimsby

# Space Poem

Stars shooting
Spaceship orbit
Meteors whistle
Gravity – none
Earth – home
Planets twinkle
ISS – shiny
Pluto – tiny.

**Nicholas Crossley (8)**
Western Primary School, Grimsby

# Adventures Of Space

The boy went in his shed,
And bumped his head.
He found a rocket,
That was as big as a giant socket.
He jumped inside,
And found some pies.
He went into space,
And found his place.
The stars were bright,
It left a path of light.
The rocket went *boom!*
As he landed on the moon.
He found an alien,
His name was Talien.
He helped him mend the ship,
Then they went on their trip.
When they landed they said goodbye,
And walked away with a great big sigh!

**Maurice Crancher (8)**
Western Primary School, Grimsby

# The Boy Went Into Space

The boy goes In hls shed
And found his rocket of red.
He blasted into the space
Like a real race.
He saw a moon
Then he waited in the afternoon.
He saw lots of stars
On the planet Mars.
Then he met an alien
His name was Zalien.
His spaceship is broken
And he needs another token.
Then the boy parachuted down to Earth
He landed on the turf.
He got his ladder
And got his spanner.
He fixed his ship
And the alien ate some chip.
Then the alien flew away
For a day.

**Alvin Lin (8)**
Western Primary School, Grimsby

# The Alien On The Moon

The boy went in his shed
And found something red.
It was a rocket
So he got the key out his pocket.
He turned the rocket's engine on
And he saw a star that shone.
He saw the planet Mars,
But there were no cars.
When he landed on the moon
He saw an alien on the moon that likes to sit upon a spoon.
There was an alien
Whose name was Taylien.
The alien's ship broke
Because there was no coke.
The boy parachuted down to Earth
And landed on grassy turf.
He climbed up his ladder
But dropped his spanner.

**Hollie Bradley (8)**
Western Primary School, Grimsby

# Space – Haiku

Colourful planets
Stars sparkling in the dark
Spacemen on the moon.

Rockets flying by
Meteors floating through space
Big and small planets.

**Joshua Essex (9)**
Western Primary School, Grimsby

# What Am I?

Planet-spinner
Star-twinkler
Moon-brightener
Space-explorer
Light-giver
Sun-riser
Sky-cleaner
Weather-changer
I'm space!

**Shannon Rose Wraith (10)**
Western Primary School, Grimsby

# Untitled

I wish I could go to the moon.
But I know that won't be soon.
One morning I saw the sky.
And came out my house to say hi.

One day I went to the Milky Way.
I know it's a name of a chocolate bar, OK.
My mum asked me if I wanted to go to Mars.
I said no and looked at the stars.

One day I saw a shooting star.
And me and my brother thought it was going afar.
And that was the end of the day.
Hooray!

**Page Marie Light (10)**
Western Primary School, Grimsby

# Out Of This World

O ut of space.
U ranus is a planet.
T ime travel to space.

O verpowered rocket.
F ire comes out of a rocket.

T here is no gravity in space.
H umans travel to space in a rocket.
I mmense planets.
S olar system is where the planets live.

W e see sparking stars when we look up in the sky.
O nly astronauts can got to space.
R ocket are fast like a cheetah.
L anding on the moon.
D ark as the night sky.

**Lewis Tuson (10)**
Western Primary School, Grimsby

# All Of The Planets

The moon is bright, can't keep light.
The moon is as bright as Heaven.
The sun is light, can't keep bright.
The sun is as hot as a boiling pot of curry.
Mars is red and dusty as a basement.
The Earth is blue because of the sea.
So the sea is all you can see.
The Earth is green because of the grass.
It's as green as an alien.
Space is huge, it won't end.
Everything will fly in the sky.
The galaxy is sparkly and beautiful.
And sometimes wonderful.

**Shannon Anastazia Lamb (10)**
Western Primary School, Grimsby

# What Am I?

Red as blood
Mysterious as a dark hole
A whole new land
Strange beings
Weird spacecrafts
Not too hot, not too cold
Amazing, beautiful landscape
Blinding view
Crazy zigzags
No human has ever set foot on me.
You can't see me if you look at the sky.
In the middle of the moon's glow.
Strange readings.
Mars!

**Phoebe Grace Turner (10)**
Western Primary School, Grimsby

# All About Space!

Stars shimmering
Spaceships fly
Meteorites crash
Gravity – float
Earth – home
ISS – noisy
Sun – fiery
Pluto – small.

**Jessica Ward (9)**
Western Primary School, Grimsby

# Space Kennings

Stars – colourful
Spaceship zooming
Meteors flash
Gravity – floating
Earth – massive
Moon – bumpy
Milky Way ring
Sun – hot
Mars – red.

**Connor Tb (9)**
Western Primary School, Grimsby

# Space Kennings

Stars shooting
Spaceship zooming
Meteors flash
Gravity – floating
Earth – massive
Moon – bumpy
Milky Way planets
Sun – hot
Mars – red.

**Charlie Piggott (8)**
Western Primary School, Grimsby

# Space Kennings

Spaceshlp zoomlng
Meteors booming
Gravity – none
Earth, planets
Stars – white
Alien – scary
Pluto – small
Sun – hot
Moon – flowing.

**Noah Freeman (9)**
Western Primary School, Grimsby

# What Am I?

Sky-lighter
Star-keeper
Oxygen-destroyer
Dust-filler
Atmosphere-maker
People-attractor
Rocket-wanter
Night-lighter.

Moon!

**Grant King (9)**
Western Primary School, Grimsby

# Planets

O ur sun is a big bright star.
U niverse is big and space is as big as the universe.
T he sun is as bright as a sunflower.

O ur Earth is big and round.
F or gravity it's a thing that would pull us to the centre of the Earth.

T he coldest planet is Pluto.
H ave a break and go to space and land on the moon.
I t's a planet. Earth is as blue and green as a leaf and the sea.
S un is a big, hot ball of fire.

W hat is space? What is the universe?
O ur planet is big.
R ound and round we spin.
L ovely space and lovely universe.
D elightful views and delightful things.

**Logan Wink (10)**
Western Primary School, Grimsby

# What Am I?

Light-less
Freezing cold
Icy diver
Colder than an ice cube, like an ice cube
Far away from the sun, lifeless
Smaller than them all, small like an ant
Rocky, hard
Smallest in the galaxy, much bigger planets
No life on there, too cold for people
Nobody has ever been there before, too far from Earth
Oxygen-destroyer, life-taker
Freezer-like, ice cube-maker.

I am Pluto!

**Callum Barraclough (10)**
Western Primary School, Grimsby

# Planets

Planets are big and some are small.
If you are stuck then you can just call.
If you are on the moon,
Then come back soon.
Planets are red.
Can you feel it on your head?
Is it bark?
Then the dogs will bark.

**Jack Dean Poland (10)**
Western Primary School, Grimsby

# Space

The boy went into his shed
That was mostly red
And found a rocket
Then looked in his pocket.

He zoomed into space
And saw Mars' ugly face
The boy dropped on the moon
With a boom.

Then met an alien
Her name was Lalian
She had a friend called Cilly
She is silly.

The boy parachuted back to Earth
And landed on a big ball of turf
He got his ladder
And took his spanner.

**Lily-Mae Scott (8)**
Western Primary School, Grimsby

# When He Saw Space

The boy went in his shed,
And found a rocket of red.
He jumped in and banged his knee,
And said, 'Eeee!'
Then he went to space,
Like it was a race.
The boy saw a shiny star,
And it was so far.
He saw the moon,
And said, 'Zoom!'
He saw a planet,
And it looked like a pomegranate.
He went boom,
And he landed like a balloon
He went to an alien,
That was called Salien.
He was sad,
And kind of mad.
The alien said hi,
And he looked in the sky.
Then he parachuted down to Earth,
And landed on a ball of turf.
He got his ladder,
And he thought it was a hammer.
He went back to the moon,
And he thought it was a spoon.
He fixed everything,
And it went zing.
Then he went back home,
But he was home alone.

**Tianna Kitatta (8)**
Western Primary School, Grimsby

# The Boy And Blue Starleem

The boy went in his shed,
And his rocket of red.
The boy flew through space,
With a smile on his face.
He landed on the moon,
In the afternoon.
He saw some stars,
But they were really far.
He met an alien,
His name was Blue Starleem.
The boy parachuted down to Earth,
And landed in a bowl of turf.
He got his tool,
He got his fuel.
He got his ladder,
He dropped his spanner.
He fixed the ships,
And did some flips.

**Mason Dodd (8)**
Western Primary School, Grimsby

# The Way Back Home

He went to go in his shed,
And found his rocket of red,
He jumped in,
With a big grin,
He shot into space,
Like it was a race,
With a zoom,
And landed on the moon,
He saw an alien,
His name was Sayn,
He landed on Earth,
And landed on a ball of turf,
He got his ladder,
And dropped his spanner,
He fixed the ships,
And gave him a wink.

**Leo Drury (7)**
Western Primary School, Grimsby

# Space

The boy went in the shed
Then he bumped his head
In the rocket he went to space
It looked like a race
Then the boy saw the moon
The boy had a spoon
He looked in his pocket
And there was a locket
He fixed his ship
And went back to Earth, quick!

**Jaden Johnson (8)**
Western Primary School, Grimsby

# In Space

The boy went in his shed,
And found a rocket of red,
He found a key in his pocket,
And jumped into the locket,
He turned the key and heard a zoom,
Before he knew it, he saw the moon,
He saw the stars twinkle in the sky,
Up near the moon where the birds don't fly,
The rocket crashed on the moon,
Everything went crash and boom,
He saw a little alien,
His name was Zalien,
He took his spanner out of his pocket,
And mended his broken red rocket,
They climbed back inside,
And went for a ride,
Off he goes back down to Earth,
His rocket landed on the turf!

**Thomas Raven (8)**
Western Primary School, Grimsby

# The Way Back Home

The spaceship ran out of fuel,
The boy got his tools and tried to fix it,
But he couldn't do it,
There was a beam of light,
That was across his sight,
He dropped his spanner and got the ladder,
He went alone back to his home,
Landed the spaceship,
And ate fish and chips.

**Latasha Craft (8)**
Western Primary School, Grimsby

# Space

Stars twinkle
Spaceships fly
Meteors boom
Gravity – none
Earth – home
Planets – big
Aliens – funny
Colours – bright
Moon – massive.

**Jasmine Tailby (8)**
Western Primary School, Grimsby

# YOUNG WRITERS INFORMATION

We hope you have enjoyed reading this book –
and that you will continue to in the coming years.

If you're a young writer who enjoys reading and
creative writing, or the parent of an enthusiastic poet or
story writer, do visit our website
www.youngwriters.co.uk. Here you will find free
competitions, workshops and games, as well as
recommended reads, a poetry glossary and our blog.

If you would like to order further copies of
this book, or any of our other titles give us
a call or visit **www.youngwriters.co.uk.**

Young Writers
Remus House
Coltsfoot Drive
Peterborough
PE2 9BF

(01733) 890066 / 898110
**info@youngwriters.co.uk**